This journal belongs to

....

RAE SIMONS

God is GOOD (All the Time)

DEVOTIONAL JOURNAL

Encouragement for Life's Ups & Downs

BARBOUR BOOKS
An Imprint of Barbour Publishing, Inc.

Our mission is to inspire the world with the life-changing message of the Bible.

 Member of the Evangelical Christian Publishers Association

Printed in China.

INTRODUCTION

Of course we all know that God is good. But sometimes it doesn't *feel* as though He is. That might not be the sort of thing we'd say out loud, but at one time or another, most of us have felt that way.

When we think like that, however, we're actually thinking about a make-believe God we've created in our own minds—a God who is an angry Judge taking note of all our faults and mistakes, a harsh Taskmaster who loves to ask things of us we don't like to do, or a faraway Deity who is indifferent to our pain and suffering. No wonder we have a hard time loving and trusting a God like that!

But that isn't the God who Jesus reveals to us through His Incarnation, a God of intimate love and tender mercy, a God who loves us no matter what, who is present with us in each sorrow and joy we experience. That is the God we are called to as followers of Jesus. That is the God we need to get to know.

Feelings come and go, of course. Some days we still may not *feel* God's presence in our lives. But the more we get to know God—as intimately and certainly as we know our closest friends—the easier we will find that we can cling to the reality that God loves us, no matter what.

Because God is good—*all the time.*

"Get to know God, and you'll be at peace."
JOB 22:21 ISV

Those who know your name trust in you, for you, Lord, have never forsaken those who seek you.
PSALM 9:10 NIV

FAITH IN GOD

"Have faith in God," Jesus answered.

MARK 11:22 NIV

When we encounter any of life's many troubles—from the small frustrations of daily life to the enormous tragedies that break our hearts—we may feel as though our faith fails us. Sometimes it just doesn't seem strong enough to handle the realities of life.

When we feel like that, though, we aren't really listening to what Jesus told His followers. Instead of having faith in God, we're trying to have faith in our own faith. And when doubts and fears overcome us, we feel that our "faith has failed." Often, we make our problems even more painful by beating ourselves up for not having more faith. We compare ourselves to others—the leaders of our church, maybe, or our friends, or the great Christian saints of history, or figures from the Bible—and our faith falls far short of what these spiritual giants seemed to possess. *No wonder God doesn't come to my help,* we may think, *when my faith is so weak and my doubts so strong.*

But that wasn't what Jesus was talking about. He didn't mean that we should have faith in our own spirituality. . .or in our insights into life's problems. . .or in the church. . .or in any human help. . .or in our ability to find an easy solution. . .or in our emotions. Those are all common mistakes we make about where we put our faith, but Jesus told us to have faith in the One who is so much greater, wiser, richer, and more loving than anything our minds can ever grasp.

Faith in God doesn't mean we always understand what is going on in our lives. It doesn't mean that our sorrow or anger, disappointment or anxiety will magically and instantly disappear. We may not see God's hand at work, and we may find little comfort in the advice of friends or in the sermons we hear at church. But none of that matters when our faith *is in God.*

Faith in God means being willing to walk in darkness sometimes. It means accepting that we don't know what's going on. And it means being willing to give even our negative emotions to Him, knowing that He is big enough to hold all our rage and sadness and frustration and fear. Nothing we feel or think diminishes Him.

He is God—and we can trust Him, no matter what, because He is always good.

....
....
....
....
....
....
....
....
....
....
....
....
....
....
....
....
....
....

THANK YOU, GOD, THAT YOU ARE BIGGER THAN ALL MY IDEAS ABOUT YOU,
BIGGER THAN ALL MY FEARS. EVEN WHEN MY TROUBLES SEEM TO
OVERWHELM ME, I PUT MY LIFE IN YOUR HANDS.

WORKED-UP FAITH

Faith comes from hearing, that is,
hearing the Good News about Christ.

ROMANS 10:17 NLT

Sometimes we feel as though we need to "work up" more faith. We act as though faith were something we could manufacture with enough determination, as though we could counteract our doubts about God's goodness with sheer willpower.

The Bible does tell us to "take every thought captive" (2 Corinthians 10:5), and psychologists remind us that our thoughts have the power to shape our realities. Think negative thoughts, and you'll probably see darkness everywhere you turn; while if you make an effort to focus on positive things, life will start to seem a bit brighter. But a positive outlook has nothing to do with faith.

Faith isn't an emotion, and it isn't something we can "work up." Instead, Paul tells us in this verse from his letter to the Romans, faith comes from hearing. We absorb faith from the voices we choose to hear, from the places where we turn our attention.

Remember when Peter tried to walk on the water? He did just fine until he stopped looking at Jesus—and then he started to sink. It's the same idea here. When our faith is small, we can enlarge it by focusing on Jesus and His Good News. As we turn our attention away from our doubts, away from our situation, away from all that is troubling us, we'll find we can hear His voice in the Scriptures. We may feel its whisper in our hearts during prayer. We might hear Him as we watch the sun set, listen to beautiful music, or gaze at a starry sky.

As the author of Hebrews wrote, when we fix our eyes on Jesus, He is the author and finisher of our faith (12:2). He doesn't need us to "work up" faith. Instead, His message to us is what plants the seeds of faith in our hearts—and that same message of love is what will help our faith to grow to maturity.

LORD, THE WATER ALL AROUND ME SEEMS AWFULLY COLD AND DEEP, AND I CAN'T HELP BUT DOUBT YOUR GOODNESS. . .BUT I'M KEEPING MY EYES ON YOU ANYWAY. DON'T LET ME SINK. I'M LISTENING FOR YOUR VOICE. PLEASE INCREASE MY FAITH.

THE MEANING OF GOD'S GOODNESS

The goodness of God endureth continually.

PSALM 52:1 KJV

"What does it mean to be good?" the Sunday school teacher asked her class of young children.

"It means you don't get in trouble," said a little boy. His expression indicated that this was an easy question with an obvious answer.

"What sort of things would get you in trouble?" the teacher asked.

"Like stealing," said one child.

"Telling lies," said another.

"Breaking your sister's toys."

"Saying mean things to people."

"So," the teacher said finally, "we might say that being good means we're kind to others and we treat them with respect. We do our best not to hurt them in any way. Now here's another question—is God good?"

The children nodded their heads. They obviously thought this was another easy question.

"Well, what does that mean?" the teacher asked. "When we say God is good, does it mean the same thing as when we say a person is good?"

This time the children looked puzzled. "No," said one child, "'cause God doesn't have to obey the rules. He's just good all the time."

"Yes, He is," the teacher agreed. "But what do we mean by that?" She waited a moment to see if anyone in the class had any more ideas, and then she said, "God doesn't need rules because He's good by His very nature. But good means good, no matter who we're talking about. So when we say that God is good, we're saying that He is kind. He doesn't want to hurt us. He loves us all the time. Everything He does, even the things we don't understand or don't like, are all done because He loves us."

"So being good is like loving," said a little girl.

The teacher smiled. "Yes, in a way. Both mean we don't put ourselves first. We do what's best for others, even when it's hard to do. The Bible's word for this is lovingkindness. And it's how God always treats us."

God's lovingkindness is what makes Him good. This is the sort of kindness that is bigger than anything we could ever do—and it's the sort of love that lasts forever. No matter what is happening in our lives, God's love will never fail us. His lovingkindness is everlasting (Psalm 136:10 NASB).

OUR TASTY GOD

Taste and see that the LORD is good.

PSALM 34:8 NLT

Sometimes the goodness of God seems so very high and far away that it doesn't even look particularly good to us, at least not in the sense in which we usually use that word. God is good—everyone knows that—but what good does His goodness do us when we can't pay our bills. . .when relationships are broken. . . or when death takes away someone we love? During times like those, God's goodness may seem too distant from us to be of any practical use.

When we talk about God being good, we often think of religion and morality. In our minds, God's goodness is the opposite of sinfulness. It's a spiritual quality, something so lofty and pure that it's beyond our ability to comprehend. While that may be true, the Greek word that our Bible translates as "good" really didn't have anything at all to do with morality or religion. According to the NAS Exhaustive Concordance, it meant simply "pleasant, agreeable, beautiful, beneficial, delightful, generous, glad, splendid, sweet." Try substituting those words for "good" in the verse from Psalms:

Taste and see that the Lord is beautiful.
Taste and see that the Lord is delightful.
Taste and see that the Lord is splendid.
Taste and see that the Lord is sweet.

When we read the verse like this, we start to realize that God's goodness is a practical thing that can be perceived by our senses. It's something we can taste in the flavors of our ordinary lives, something we can see amid the colors and shadows of daily life. Even on the bleakest days, when nothing seems to be going right, God wants us to see His beauty in the sunrise; He wants us to perceive His delightfulness in a child's face; He wants our hearts to be lightened when we experience the splendor of music; and He wants us to taste His sweetness in each meal we eat.

God's goodness is woven through our lives, in countless ordinary ways. We just have to pay attention.

. . . .

. . . .

. . . .

. . . .

. . . .

. . . .

. . . .

. . . .

. . . .

. . . .

. . . .

. . . .

. . . .

. . . .

. . . .

. . . .

. . . .

JESUS, EVEN WHEN MY HEART IS TROUBLED AND MY MIND
PREOCCUPIED WITH WORRIES, REMIND ME TO SEE AND
TASTE GOD'S GOODNESS WITH MY PHYSICAL SENSES.

GOD'S NAME

Those who know your name trust in you.

PSALM 9:10 NLT

Do you know what God's name is? We use the word *God* so easily, but do we stop to think what we really mean by that? How do you know that when you use the word that you really mean the same thing as your friend does when she talks about God? Maybe God is whoever and whatever we think He is. . . .

The Bible, however, tells us quite a bit about God's name, and in Bible language, *name* often refers to character. In many early cultures, including the biblical world, names were powerful things. True names weren't given arbitrarily, but instead, they revealed something important about the character or work of the person to which they referred.

The names of God given to us in the Bible tell us who He really is. They show us His love, wisdom, power, grace—and goodness. They tell us that it's safe to put our trust in Him. He's not some make-believe Being we've created in our own heads, and His nature doesn't depend on our personal beliefs about Him.

When God spoke to Moses from the burning bush, He told Moses that His name is "I AM" (Exodus 3:14). That is a strange sort of name, granted, one that we humans have struggled to understand down through the centuries. It tells us some basic and essential things about God, however.

First of all, it tells us that God is a reality, not a subjective belief or opinion. Although we may not be able to truly grasp who He is, He is *real*, an objective, factual God who is not dependent on our ideas or devotion to give Him substance. He is who He is.

What's more, the words "I AM" tell us that God exists always in the present tense, unchanged by passing time or human fashions. He is who He is yesterday, today, and forever. His nature is eternal. In the book of Revelation, Jesus said, "I am the Alpha and the Omega—the beginning and the end. . . . I am the one who is, who always was, and who is still to come" (Revelation 1:8 NLT). God's most essential name—I AM—tells us that He is greater than time.

This mysterious name also tells us that we cannot put God into a tidy box we've created for Him. He's simply too great for that. When we truly know God's name, though, even if we can't understand it, we know we can trust Him, all the time and even beyond time.

I DO NOT UNDERSTAND WHO YOU ARE, GOD, BUT REMIND ME NOT TO CONFUSE
UNDERSTANDING WITH FAITH. HELP ME TO TRUST THE GREAT I AM.

GOD'S BLANK CHECK

The name of the LORD is a strong tower; a righteous person
rushes to it and is lifted up above the danger.

PROVERBS 18:10 ISV

When the Israelites asked Moses, "What is your God's name?" they meant, "Who and what is this God of whom you speak? What is His character? What is He like? What does He do? Exactly what sort of a being is He?"

If we don't understand the meaning of God's name, we'll have a hard time trusting Him through all the challenges of our lives. When we don't really know who God is, we find it hard to believe that God is truly good. After all, the world is full of terrible suffering and horrifying violence. How could a good God allow those things to exist?

The name God gave to Moses—I AM—seems a bit unfinished. But throughout the pages of the Bible, the meaning is filled in. According to Hannah Whitall Smith, author of *The Christian's Secret of a Happy Life*, the name I AM "includes everything the human heart longs for and needs." She goes on to say:

> *This unfinished name of God seems to me like a blank check signed by a rich friend given to us to be filled in with whatever sum we may desire. The whole Bible tells us what it means. Every attribute of God, every revelation of His character, every proof of His undying love, every declaration of His watchful care, every assertion of His purposes of tender mercy, every manifestation of His loving kindness—all are the filling out of this unfinished "I am.". . . This apparently unfinished name, therefore, is the most comforting name the heart of man could devise, because it allows us to add to it, without any limitation, whatever we feel the need of, and even "exceeding abundantly" beyond all that we can ask or think.[1]*

Smith also reminds us that "if our hearts are full of our own wretched 'I ams' we will have no ears to hear His glorious, soul-satisfying 'I am.'" By this she means that all our negative self-talk *I am so stupid, I am so weak, I am such a failure*—get in the way of our understanding of God's magnificent I AM, a blank check of loving abundance upon which we can draw, no matter our need.

---

[1] Hannah Whitall Smith, *The God of All Comfort* (Uhrichsville, OH: Barbour Publishing, Inc., 2013).

....
....
....
....
....
....
....
....
....
....
....
....
....
....
....
....
....
....

THANK YOU, LOVING GOD, THAT YOUR NAME IS A BLANK CHECK,
GRANTING ME THE INFINITE RICHES OF YOUR LOVE.

JESUS SHOWS US THE GOODNESS OF THE FATHER

Anyone who has seen me has seen the Father.

JOHN 14:9 NIV

The personality and character of Jesus completes the I AM God gave Moses so many centuries earlier. Jesus translates the name of God into a language we can more easily understand. He reveals to us the invisible Creator of the universe. If any ideas we have about God are contrary to what we see in Jesus, then we need to let go of those thoughts and ask Jesus to replace them with the Truth of His Being.

What's more, Jesus explicitly filled in the Old Testament blank-check name of I AM. Here are just a few of the "I am" statements He made that are recorded in the Gospel of John:

"I am the bread of life; he who comes to Me will not hunger, and he who believes in Me will never thirst." (John 6:35 NASB)

"I am the Light of the world; he who follows Me will not walk in the darkness, but will have the Light of life." (John 8:12 NASB)

"I am the door; if anyone enters through Me, he will be saved, and will go in and out and find pasture. . . . I came that they may have life, and have it abundantly." (John 10:9–10 NASB)

"I am the good shepherd, and I know My own and My own know Me, even as the Father knows Me and I know the Father; and I lay down My life for the sheep." (John 10:14–15 NASB)

"I am the resurrection and the life; he who believes in Me will live even if he dies." (John 11:25 NASB)

These verses show us a God who fills our hunger, sheds light into our darkness, opens up new opportunities, lays down His own life for us, and gives us endless abundant life. Nowhere in all the Gospels does Jesus ever say, "I am a stern and cruel Taskmaster!" Nor does He say, "I am far away from people, and I do not care about their suffering." Instead, Jesus shows us again and again a God who is good and loving—all the time.

....
....
....
....
....
....
....
....
....
....
....
....
....
....
....
....
....

WHEN I AM FILLED WITH DOUBT AND FEAR, LORD JESUS,
SHOW ME YOUR FACE. REMIND ME THAT YOU
ARE THE TRANSLATION OF GOD'S LOVE

GOD OF ALL COMFORT

Praise be to the God and Father of our Lord Jesus Christ, the Father of compassion and the God of all comfort, who comforts us in all our troubles.

2 CORINTHIANS 1:3–4 NIV

Among all the names that the Bible gives us for God, "God of all comfort" is one of the most beautiful. It tells us that God's love and concern reach into our lives, with all their troubles and tribulations, and gives us the encouragement and strength we need.

The word *all* is an important part of this name. "God of comfort" would still be a lovely name, but "all" makes the comfort God gives us even fuller, wider, and deeper. The Greek word used here in the original scripture implies a wealth of meaning: *everything required for wholeness, all respects, entire, always and forever.* God's comfort can't be limited; no condition in our life can deduct from its fullness.

What's more, the Greek word that our Bible versions translate as "comfort" has an even deeper meaning than the English word. Literally, it means "an intimate call, a close-up and personal urging." In fact, it's the same word that's often used in the New Testament to refer to the Holy Spirit—the Paraclete, the Comforter. In other words, the God of all comfort comes to us through the constant and intimate companionship of His Spirit, walking close beside us through all the moments of our lives.

When I hear the word *comfort*, I think of my slippers. At the end of a long workday, when I've been on my feet in shoes that pinch, it's such a relief to come home and slip my cold, tired feet into my warm, soft slippers. That tiny, ordinary moment symbolizes for me all the relief and comfort of homecoming after a hard day.

And this prosaic, practical comfort is also a part of God's nature. As God's people, we aren't guaranteed freedom from problems. Our outer lives will always be filled with challenges, great and small. But despite that, our inner lives can be lived in comfort—the fathomless, bountiful, intimate comfort of God that enfolds all our trials and pain the way soft slippers enfold tired feet. "As a mother comforts her child," God says to us in the book of Isaiah, "so will I comfort you; and you will be comforted" (66:13 NIV).

....
....
....
....
....
....
....
....
....
....
....
....
....
....
....
....
....
....
....
....

THANK YOU, GOD, THAT YOU ARE MY COMFORTER. TEACH ME TO RUN TO
YOU WHENEVER I AM SAD OR FRIGHTENED, THE WAY I ONCE RAN TO MY
MOTHER, KNOWING THAT I COULD FIND ALL COMFORT IN HER ARMS.

OUR FATHOMLESS GOD

Thou, whose name alone is JEHOVAH,
art the most high over all the earth.

PSALM 83:18 KJV

The word *Jehovah* is often used in the Old Testament to express the I AM, the self-existing One who is and was and will be, world without end. Some versions of the Bible translate Jehovah as "Yahweh," while others simply use the word *Lord. The Brown-Driver-Briggs Hebrew and English Lexicon* says that Jehovah is the "proper name of the God of Israel," and that it means "the One who brings into being," "the Life-Giver," "the One who is," "the Ever-Living One"—mysterious, intriguing names that remind us that God is beyond our ability to ever truly grasp with our human minds. He is far too great to be contained by any box we fashion for Him.

"The Most High" is another name used in the Bible for God. It tells us that God's viewpoint is far above ours. He sees our lives in their entirety, as though He were looking down at them from a mountaintop or an airplane. He is supreme. Nothing is loftier than He is.

Now take into consideration this: this lofty, fathomless, always-alive Being became visible to human beings through Jesus of Nazareth, and now His Spirit enters into our inmost selves. He invites us to experience an intimate relationship with Him. He comes to us in every moment of our lives. It seems unbelievable, and yet the Bible assures us over and over that this is true. When our lives are filled with troubles, this relationship allows us to look at our circumstances from a higher perspective—the perspective of the Life-Giver who never dies.

So the next time life seems overwhelming, remind yourself who God really is. His presence is real in our lives, an immense and precious resource we so often forget to utilize. His power is greater than any financial difficulty, His love is deeper than any human criticism we can face, and His wisdom is wider than any confusion we experience. Why not avail yourself of His power, love, and wisdom?

No matter what is happening in your life right now, God is there—and He longs to help you.

MOST HIGH GOD, THANK YOU FOR LOVING ME. I PLACE ALL MY PROBLEMS IN YOUR HANDS, TRUSTING YOU TO WORK THROUGH THEM ALL TO BRING HEALING AND WHOLENESS TO MY HEART AND TO THE WORLD AROUND ME.

THE LORD WILL PROVIDE

Abraham named the place Yahweh-Yireh
(which means "the LORD will provide").
GENESIS 22:14 NLT

Here and there in the Old Testament, the meaning of "Yahweh" (Jehovah) is filled in with some extra words. In this case, after God gave Abraham a ram to sacrifice in place of his son Isaac, Abraham referred to the place where it happened as "the Lord will provide." This father of our faith had realized that one of the characteristics of his God was that He sees the needs of His people—and He provides what is needed.

Jesus reinforced this understanding throughout the Gospels. "Your Father knows exactly what you need even before you ask him!" He told His followers "So don't worry about these things, saying, 'What will we eat? What will we drink? What will we wear?'. . . Seek the Kingdom of God above all else, and live righteously, and he will give you everything you need" (Matthew 6:8, 31, 33 NLT).

In the book of Philippians, Paul expands on this, saying, "And my God will supply all your needs according to His riches in glory in Christ Jesus" (4:19 NASB). Paul is reminding us here that God—Jehovah, the Ever-Living One—can draw on His infinite abundance to fulfill our needs. No limitation hampers His generosity and love.

Of course, we sometimes don't *feel* as though that's the case. Why, we wonder, can't God use all those riches in glory to pay our mortgage. . .get us a promotion at work. . .heal our bodies. . .or mend our broken hearts? But God asks us to trust Him. He asks us to believe that He truly sees and understands our needs, better than we do ourselves.

We can have confidence that He is not ignoring us, even when we feel as though we're drowning in troubles. Instead, He is all the while meeting our needs, unfolding the deepest desires of our hearts—if we can only have the patience to wait and seek Him first, before any of our selfish concerns.

God created us, and He knows the very essence of who we are—body, mind, and soul—infinitely more than we can ever know ourselves. He knows what is truly best for us and what would not be good for us, just as good parents know that no matter how good candy bars and cookies taste, what their children *really* need is a balanced diet of fruit and vegetables, protein, and complex carbohydrates. God knows what we need, and He will provide.

....

....

....

....

....

....

....

....

....

....

....

....

....

....

....

....

HEAVENLY FATHER, THANK YOU THAT YOU KNOW MY NEEDS BETTER THAN
I KNOW THEM—AND THAT RIGHT NOW, YOU ARE WORKING TO MEET THEM.

THE LORD IS MY BANNER

*Moses built an altar there and named it Yahweh-Nissi
(which means "the LORD is my banner").*

EXODUS 17:15 NLT

"The Lord is my banner" was another name that Moses used to describe Yahweh. By this, Moses meant that God is like the flag that an army carried when it marched into battle. This banner served as a rallying point for the troops. If they were scattered during the fight, they would make their way back to the flag that was flying high in the sky, showing them which way to go. When defeat seemed certain, the warriors' hearts would lift whenever they saw that bright ripple of fabric, reassuring them that their leader was still fighting with them.

God is like that. He fights with us in all our battles. We catch a glimpse of His love, shining like a bright pennant, and we are encouraged. If we lose our way, His presence guides us back amid all the chaos and darkness of the battleground.

The Bible tells us this over and over within its pages. In 2 Chronicles, we read, "Thus saith the LORD unto you, Be not afraid nor dismayed by reason of this great multitude; for the battle is not yours, but God's" (20:15 KJV). The psalmist wrote, "Some trust in chariots, and some in horses: but we will remember the name of the LORD our God" (20:7 KJV).

The Bible may have been referring to actual battlegrounds, where men with weapons clashed against each other from horseback and chariots, but God's power is equally effective in all the modern-day combat zones we encounter. His banner flies over us when we face a conflict at work; His flag is lifted up in the midst of family arguments; and we can catch sight of His pennant when we struggle to endure another day of physical pain and weakness. Always, in each battle we face, His banner over us is love (Song of Solomon 2:4).

Soldiers in Bible times knew that the battlefield was not a place where every man fought for himself. If that were the case, the fight would have quickly disintegrated into chaos. Instead, they were organized around their leader, the one who carried the banner. They counted on him to lead the battle to victory. Their part was to trust his guidance and follow him.

....

....

....

....

....

....

....

....

....

....

....

....

....

....

....

HELP ME TO REMEMBER, LORD, THAT I DO NOT HAVE TO FIGHT MY BATTLES ALONE.
REMIND ME TO LOOK FOR YOUR BANNER—AND FOLLOW YOU.

GOD'S NAME IS PEACE

Gideon built an altar to the LORD there and named it Yahweh-Shalom (which means "the LORD is peace").

JUDGES 6:24 NLT

Gideon spoke the name of Yahweh-Shalom—"the Lord is peace"—after an encounter he had with the Living God on the eve of a great battle with the Midianites. The battle had not yet been fought, and no victories had been won, but with the eye of faith, Gideon saw the peace that God promised. Despite the external conflicts that still needed to be overcome, Gideon had fought the internal battle against doubt. He was at peace *now*, even as he prepared for the fight.

Unlike Gideon, we often make the mistake of thinking that we must have external peace before we can experience inner peace. We think, *If only all this turmoil around me—at work, in my home, in our nation, in the entire world—would cease, then I could finally know peace.* But God wants to give us a real and lasting inner peace in the midst of all the uproar in our lives.

This is the peace Jesus promised in the Gospels. "I am leaving you with a gift," he said, "peace of mind and heart. And the peace I give is a gift the world cannot give. So don't be troubled or afraid" (John 14:27 NLT). It's the peace that Paul prayed would be granted to the Thessalonians: "Now may the Lord of peace himself give you peace at all times and in every way" (2 Thessalonians 3:16 NIV).

God is real and present in our lives *all the time, no matter what*—and that means that the aspect of God's nature that is peace is also available to us *all the time, no matter what*. This is a reality that remains constant, regardless of how much outer conflict we are experiencing at the moment.

Just as there are times when clouds hide the sun's constant presence from our eyes, we all have times when life's storms hide God's peace from our senses. The Apostle Paul tells us the secret to clear seeing: "Be careful for nothing; but in everything by prayer and supplication with thanksgiving let your requests be made known unto God. And the peace of God, which passeth all understanding, shall keep your hearts and minds through Christ Jesus" (Philippians 4:6–7 KJV). In other words, instead of worrying and dwelling on your troubles, hand them over to God—and He'll give you His peace in return!

....
....
....
....
....
....
....
....
....
....
....
....
....
....
....
....

GOD OF PEACE, I GIVE YOU ALL THAT IS IN TURMOIL IN MY LIFE RIGHT NOW.
FILL MY HEART WITH YOUR PEACE, EVEN AS YOU WORK YOUR
WILL IN ALL THESE CIRCUMSTANCES.

GOD IS THERE

From that day the name of the city will be "The LORD Is There."

EZEKIEL 48:35 NLT

The prophet Ezekiel used the name Jehovah-shammah— "the Lord is there"— when he was shown in a vision, during the twenty-fifth year of the Israelites' captivity in Babylon, what was to be their future home. This vision was detailed and specific, describing exact measurements and locations of buildings and land. In the present moment, the Israelites were still captives, far from their homeland. At the same time, however, Ezekiel knew that the vision had revealed to him a reality.

We are in a similar situation. We live in captivity to the weakness of our bodies, the darkness of this world, the confusion of our thoughts and emotions—and yet at the same time, we can experience the reality of God's goodness in our lives. God is there. This is the most basic quality of God's nature: His presence is always with us.

Again and again throughout the Bible, God promises His presence. "I will be with you," He told Moses (Exodus 3:12). "I will be with him in trouble," He told the psalmist (91:15), and to the prophet Isaiah He said, "When you pass through the waters, I will be with you" (43:2). God really didn't need to say anything more. His presence is all we need. It's the guarantee that all our needs will be supplied. It's the promise that we are safe. Within God's presence are all the other qualities of His nature: love, abundance, peace, goodness.

Jesus also bore this same name. When the angel of the Lord announced to Joseph the coming birth of Christ, he said: "They shall call his name Emmanuel, which being interpreted is, God with us" (Matthew 1:23 KJV). Jesus' very identity tells us that God, the Almighty, the Creator of heaven and earth, is with us.

These two names, Jehovah-shammah and Emmanuel, mean the same thing: that God is surrounding and sustaining everything, present with us, even on our darkest days. The psalmist wrote: "Whither shall I go from thy spirit? Or whither shall I flee from thy presence? If I ascend up into heaven, thou art there: if I make my bed in hell, behold, thou art there. If I take the wings of the morning, and dwell in the uttermost parts of the sea; even there shall thy hand lead me, and thy right hand shall hold me" (139:7–10).

....
....
....
....
....
....
....
....
....
....
....
....
....
....
....
....
....
....
....
....

THANK YOU, LORD, THAT YOU ARE PRESENT IN MY LIFE.

TRIALS

Dear friends, don't be surprised at the fiery trials you are going through, as if something strange were happening to you. Instead, be very glad—because these trials will make you partners with Christ in his suffering, so that you will have the wonderful joy of seeing his glory when it is revealed to all the world.

1 PETER 4:12-13 NLT

These verses tell us that trials are normal. Everyone, even the great heroes of the early church, faces hard times. And yet somehow, we always think life should go along smoothly. When it doesn't, when a problem comes along—an illness, a financial problem, a family conflict, or whatever—we act as though it was something strange. It hits us hard. We're surprised that something like this could happen.

God may not seem very good when we're in the midst of trouble. Oh sure, we know with our heads that God is supposed to be good—but how good is someone who allows bad things to happen to the people He's supposed to love? Being "very glad" in the middle of trials seems just plain silly. And yet that's what Peter wrote. Through suffering, he said, we become partners with Christ. Paul also talked about "what it means to share in his sufferings" (Philippians 3:10 ISV).

This is a hard concept to grasp. It may help if we think about a friend who shared with us a particularly hard time in our lives; afterward, our friendship moved to a new and deeper level. Suffering drew us together.

So when trials come—and they always do, sooner or later—we can be glad for the opportunity to grow closer to Jesus. Through each problem, we can learn to know Him better. And then, with the psalmist, we can say to Him, "You will show me the way of life, granting me the joy of your presence and the pleasures of living with you forever" (Psalm 16:11 NLT).

With each trial, we will learn—with heart knowledge rather than head knowledge—that God's goodness is able to transform the most difficult situations. He will always take care of us and supply our needs—and so we don't need to worry about today's trials. We will have learned to have confidence that our God is good.

....

....

....

....

....

....

....

....

....

....

....

....

....

....

....

....

....

....

....

WHEN I DOUBT YOUR GOODNESS, JESUS, DRAW ME CLOSER TO YOU. MAY I COME
TO KNOW YOU SO WELL THAT I CAN REJOICE EVEN IN THE MIDST OF TRIALS.

SAVED!

"Behold, God is my salvation, I will trust and not be afraid; For the LORD GOD is my strength and song, And He has become my salvation."

ISAIAH 12:2 NASB

Evangelical Christians speak of "being saved." "Salvation" is a sort of code word for those who have committed their lives to Jesus. The word has become so familiar that sometimes we forget the depth of meaning that lay behind the original word when it was used in the scriptures.

This verse from Isaiah tells us that God *is* our salvation. That is His identity. And because we know that God is eternal and never-changing, salvation is who He is *all the time.* That never changes. Our anxieties and doubts and fears can't change it. If our car breaks down three times in one month, God is still our salvation; if we're ill week after week, God is still our salvation; and when we argue day after day with our husband and we wonder if this time our marriage will survive, God is even then our salvation.

What does that mean, though? When the prophet Isaiah said that God was his salvation, what was he trying to say? The Hebrew word used in this verse was *yeshuah.* According to the *NAS Exhaustive Concordance,* this word means "deliverance from danger; safety; prosperity and well-being; victory."

We could rewrite this verse like this: "God delivers me from danger. He is my prosperity, my well-being. He gives me victory." If we can truly believe that those statements are fact, we no longer need to be afraid, no matter how many problems we encounter. We can trust that God will bring victory and deliverance. He is our safety and our well-being.

Our physical, emotional, or spiritual weakness won't get in God's way. We don't need to try to be stronger than we are—because God is our strength. And we don't need to work hard to have positive emotions—because God is our song. He is our salvation.

And that Hebrew word that means salvation, *yeshuah*? That also happens to be the Hebrew name for Jesus! Jesus' name is salvation—rescue, deliverance, well-being, safety. That's who He is.

....

....

....

....

....

....

....

....

....

....

....

....

....

....

....

....

....

JESUS, THANK YOU THAT YOU ARE MY DELIVERANCE.
YOU RESCUE ME FROM ALL THE DANGERS I FACE.

THE COMFORTER

The Comforter, which is the Holy Ghost, whom the
Father will send in my name, he shall teach you all things.

JOHN 14:26 KJV

As Christians, most of us are familiar with the concept of the Trinity—God in three persons, Father, Son, and Holy Spirit. When everything in our lives seems to be falling apart, though, thinking about the Trinity may not seem very relevant. If our children are in trouble at school, our husband has lost his job, or our basement is flooded, thinking about a difficult theological concept like the Trinity may seem pretty pointless.

But we don't need to understand the theology to experience the presence of the third person of the Trinity in our lives. When Jesus promised His followers that God would send them the Holy Spirit, He was telling them about something real and practical that would change their lives.

The Greek word that the King James Version translates as "Comforter" can also mean "Helper," "Advocate," "Counselor," or "Companion." It referred to someone who would enter intimately into the situation, someone with deep insight and wisdom who would be able to not only comfort but also give sound advice and guidance, someone who would know us intimately and be able to speak up on our behalf.

This aspect of God's nature is pretty amazing if you think about it. The living Sprit of the Creator of the universe is present all the time in our lives. There is nothing we need to do to earn that Presence. There is no special prayer or magical formula for calling the Holy Spirit to enter our lives—the Spirit is already there, within us and all around us. Our Comforter is not far off in heaven where we cannot find Him. He is close at hand. He doesn't come and go, but rather He abides with us constantly.

When life is going well, it's easier to believe that the Comforter is present in our lives. We need the Holy Spirit even more when everything seems to be going wrong, and yet in our minds, we twist the promises in the scriptures, acting as though we believe exactly the opposite from what they actually state. When we read Paul's statement that "God comforts the downcast" (2 Corinthians 7:6), we seem to secretly believe that he said, "God forsakes those who are downcast."

But that's just not the case! Instead, God's Spirit of comfort is always there. He will never leave us or forsake us.

....
....
....
....
....
....
....
....
....
....
....
....
....
....
....
....
....
....

HOLY SPIRIT, HELP ME. . .TEACH ME. . .GUIDE ME. . .COMFORT ME.

YOU HAVE NOT BEEN ABANDONED

"In Your great compassion You did not make an end of them or forsake them, For You are a gracious and compassionate God. Now therefore, our God, the great, the mighty, and the awesome God, who keeps covenant and lovingkindness, Do not let all the hardship seem insignificant before You, Which has come upon us. . . . Behold, we are slaves today. . . . We are in great distress."

NEHEMIAH 9:31–32, 36–37 NASB

The stories in the Bible make it clear that human beings have always gone through times when they felt as though God had abandoned them. They looked around, and all they saw were troubles. How could God still be present in their lives when everywhere they turned they saw only hardship and distress?

The next time you feel like this, try reading what God told Israel when the people were feeling abandoned by their God: "Listen to Me and pay attention. I called you when you were still inside your mother's body. I named you, and I said to you, You are Mine. I will use you to show the world My beauty" (Isaiah 49: 1, 3, paraphrased).

"But," you might respond, "everything I've done has just been a waste of time and energy. I haven't managed to accomplish anything" (v. 4).

And God answers, "I will make you a light to shine into the world, so that others will see in you My salvation" (v. 6).

"But no one likes me," you say (v. 7). "Everyone looks down on me and criticizes me."

"Nevertheless," says God, "I chose you" (v. 7). And then He goes on to say, "I will rescue you. I will help you. I will keep you safe. Your very life will be a promise that others can see. The entire earth will rejoice because of what God is going to do in your life. The sky and the mountains will shout for joy and burst into song—because God will comfort you" (vv. 9, 13).

"But," you say, "it feels as though You've forsaken me. I feel like You've forgotten all about me" (v. 14).

And then God smiles. "Could a mother forget her baby? Even if she could, I could never forget you. I've written your name on the palms of My hands. I'm always thinking about you. Everything that has injured you will come to an end, I promise, and you're going to feel like a bride on her wedding day" (vv. 15–16, 18).

GOD, WHEN I FEEL ABANDONED, REMIND ME THAT
MY NAME IS WRITTEN ON YOUR HANDS.

EVERYTHING IS POSSIBLE!

Jesus looked at them intently and said, "Humanly speaking,
it is impossible. But not with God. Everything is possible with God."
MARK 10:27 NLT

We often limit what God can do in our lives with our ideas about what is possible and what isn't. But the Bible makes clear that we need to let go of those ideas. God can do the impossible.

Millennia ago, God told Abraham to go outdoors and "look up at the sky and count the stars—if indeed you can count them" (Genesis 15:5 NIV). Then God made an impossible promise to Abraham: "So shall your offspring be." Abraham knew that what God said was impossible because he had no children at all, and he and his wife were too old to conceive a child.

And yet Abraham believed God's promise—and God did the impossible. When Abraham was one hundred and his wife Sarah was ninety, their son Isaac was born. Isaac was the beginning of the Jewish people, who now are more than can be counted.

The prophet Jeremiah had to learn the same lesson Abraham did, the same lesson we too have to learn and relearn. "I prayed to the LORD," Jeremiah wrote, "saying, 'Ah Lord GOD! Behold, You have made the heavens and the earth by Your great power and by Your outstretched arm! Nothing is too difficult for You.' . . . Then the word of the LORD came to Jeremiah, saying, 'Behold, I am the LORD, the God of all flesh; is anything too difficult for Me?'" (Jeremiah 32:16–17, 26–27 NASB).

God makes a habit of doing the impossible. Enemies' walls fall down when people blow trumpets. Those with lifelong disabilities are healed. Dead men rise up and live. And the virgin gives birth to God's Son.

We can't predict what God will do in the impossible situations of our own lives. But we do know that He won't be limited by what is "possible." If it's hard for you to believe that right now, try looking up at the stars some night soon. The same God who made those distant blazing balls of gas is present in your circumstances. He can do the impossible.

....

....

....

....

....

....

....

....

....

....

....

....

....

....

....

....

STAR-CREATOR, REMIND ME NOT TO PLACE LIMITS ON WHAT YOU CAN DO IN MY LIFE.

GOD'S GRACE

Isn't everything you have and everything you are sheer gifts from God? . . . You already have all you need.

1 CORINTHIANS 4:7–8 MSG

The word that's translated as "grace" in our English New Testament is a Greek word that was connected to joyful rejoicing; it also implied sweetness, loveliness, favor, goodwill, and kindness. The word occurs in the New Testament Greek at least 170 times, so we know grace was an important concept to the early followers of Jesus. Meanwhile, in the Old Testament Hebrew Bible, the word translated as grace also had to do with loveliness, but more often it implied "favor," an act of blessing. Old Testament grace was not something abstract and hazy; it was something active that rolled up its sleeves and got to work, making the world a better place.

Throughout the Bible, grace is something that connects God's heart and ours. It is powerful; it changes both our inner and outer lives. It is something that "labored" in the apostle Paul's life, allowing him to grow spiritually while he accomplished great things for God. Grace is something that makes us strong enough to face the challenges of our days (2 Corinthians 12:9). It is the Spirit of God present in our lives (Hebrews 10:29). God's grace is tied up in a package with His mercy, compassion, and goodness (Psalm 145:8–9).

If we have eyes to see, we'll find God's grace everywhere we turn. Grace shines in the sunlight; it touches our lives through a neighbor's smile or a child's laughter; it warms our hearts in acts of unexpected kindness from a passing stranger. And we also find it inside our own hearts. It is the capacity to be kind when we thought we'd used up all our patience; it is the strength we find inside ourselves to make a change for the good; it is our ability to love someone who has hurt us.

Always, God's grace is something that is freely given. There is nothing we can do to earn it. It just shows up in our lives, undeserved. It is the expression of divine goodness, flowing into our lives. In the words written by the author of Hebrews, "Let us therefore come boldly unto the throne of grace, that we may obtain mercy, and find grace to help in time of need" (4:16 KJV).

....

....

....

....

....

....

....

....

....

....

....

....

....

....

....

....

GOD OF GRACE, THANK YOU FOR ALL THE GIFTS YOU HAVE
SHOWERED ON ME. I PRAISE YOU FOR YOUR GOODNESS.

SHOWERS OF BLESSING

Let my teaching fall on you like rain; let my speech settle like dew. Let my words fall like rain on tender grass, like gentle showers on young plants.

DEUTERONOMY 32:2 NLT

When life gets busy, when we're juggling responsibilities and facing conflicts everywhere we turn, we may find ourselves plodding through life as though it were an endurance test. We need to take time to pause for a moment and listen to God's Spirit teaching our hearts. Otherwise, we'll miss many of the good things God longs for us to have. We'll overlook the small joys and tiny blessings He showers constantly into our lives.

But I'm too busy to stop right now, you may be thinking. *Let me wait till this project has been completed. . .until my mother is out of the hospital. . .until the kids are back in school. . .until life isn't so hectic. Let me wait until things get back to normal.*

Thinking like that, though, means we will always be postponing the time when we reassess our lives—because face it, there's always *something* going on in our lives. We need to accept that "normal" is right now, this present moment with all its demands. And it's here, in the midst of the busyness, that God wants to shower us with His goodness.

Most of us are familiar with the Beatitudes, those words that Jesus spoke in one of His sermons. Try reading them again, though, with your own life's situation in your mind. It might sound something like this:

God blesses you when you aren't sure how you're going to pay your bills, for the Kingdom of God is yours. God blesses you when you long for something more in life, for you will be satisfied. God blesses you when life beats you down and makes you cry, for in due time you will laugh. When you feel lonely and excluded, be happy! Yes, leap for joy! For God has something even better He wants to give you. (Luke 6:20–23, paraphrased)

No matter how busy your day is, take time today to listen to the voice of Jesus. His words will fall on you like a gentle rain, refreshing your tired heart and spilling over into blessing all you do.

44

DEAR JESUS, REMIND ME TO TAKE TIME TO HEAR YOU, TODAY AND EVERY DAY.
GIVE ME SHARPER EARS, SO THAT I CAN HEAR YOU SPEAKING TO MY
HEART, AND CLEAR VISION, SO I CAN SEE YOUR BLESSINGS.

COUNTING OUR BLESSINGS

*Surely you have granted him unending blessings
and made him glad with the joy of your presence.*

PSALM 21:6 NIV

"Count your blessings," the old hymn says, "name them one by one; and it will surprise you what the Lord hath done."

Paying attention to the blessings in our lives doesn't always come naturally, though. It's easier to notice all the hard things, the wrong things, the painful things. God doesn't seem very good when our perspective is skewed to notice only the negatives!

"Counting our blessings" may seem like a tired old saying—but it's actually a practical strategy for adjusting our vision so we can once more see the goodness of God. Psychological studies have even found that people who write down a daily list of the good things in their lives are not only happier than people who instead list the frustrations and challenges in their lives, but they are also physically healthier. They have more physical and emotional energy to face their lives.

When we count our blessings, God blesses us even more! As we say thank You to God, He heaps blessing upon blessing into our lives.

Try it yourself. For a week, take five minutes every day to write down all the blessings that came to you in the last twenty-four hours. A blessing might be something as simple as:

- Taking a walk with your dog.
- Talking over a cup of coffee with a close friend.
- A quiet dinner with your husband.
- A hot bath.
- A book you've been wanting to read.
- A moment of quiet prayer.
- A special Bible verse.
- An orange-streaked sky or a silver moon.
- Exchanging a friendly smile with a stranger.
- Listening to music you love.
- A favorite television show.
- The first snowfall, the first flowers of spring, or the first scarlet leaves on the trees.
- A good night's sleep.
- Waking up next to the man you love.

Keeping a "gratitude journal" is a way to cultivate a greater awareness of God's goodness.

THANK YOU, GOD, FOR THE BOUNTIFUL
BLESSINGS YOU POUR INTO MY LIFE.

WAITING FOR GOD

The eyes of all wait upon thee; and thou givest them their meat in due season.

PSALM 145:15 KJV

I hate to wait. Waiting seems to me like wasted time, like passive, empty time that *should* be spent being active. Whether I'm stuck in traffic, waiting on hold during a phone call, or standing in line at the department of motor vehicles, the longer I wait, the more frustrated and impatient I feel.

I'm just as bad when it comes to waiting for bigger things, like the end of a long illness, the homecoming of an adult child who lives on the other side of the country, or the resolution of an ongoing conflict with my husband. If I don't have something *right now*, I feel as though I'll *never* have it. Life seems to have an empty hole in it.

But God sees from a perspective outside time. We see an example of this in the Old Testament, when He commanded the people of Israel to count their harvest, beginning the day after the Sabbath during Passover (Leviticus 23:15). For nearly two thousand years, the Jewish people had no homeland, and they had no harvest to count—and yet they continued to obey this Old Testament commandment. They counted a harvest that from the world's perspective simply didn't exist. But they counted it as an act of faith. Along the same lines, we're told in the New Testament that faith is having "confidence in what we hope for and assurance about what we do not see" (Hebrews 11:1 NIV).

This means that when I'm tired of waiting, I can be like the Jewish people and count a harvest that's yet to come. Whether it's healing for that long illness, the longed-for homecoming of my child, or the resolution of the conflict with my husband, I can be grateful for the blessing that waits to be revealed.

We don't always know how God will bless us—but we know God is good, and He *will* bless.

SECOND CHANCES

*I am certain that God, who began the good work
within you, will continue his work until it is finally
finished on the day when Christ Jesus returns.*

PHILIPPIANS 1:6 NLT

If we don't trust God, we won't be able to believe in His goodness. We may say that we believe God is good—but our emotions tell us something else. Deep inside, we believe God is frightening or faraway. We think He either won't do anything to help us, or He will actively do something to hurt us.

The Bible makes clear that trust is essential to our relationship with God. It's also essential to our relationships with other people. It's a psychological necessity for a happy and healthy life.

Most of us learned to trust as babies; we cried, and our parents came to our aid, teaching us that we could count on them to be there when we needed them. That most basic level of trust was the foundation on which all our human relationships were built. It is also what makes us able to trust God.

But sometimes parents fail to teach their children how to trust. If our parents hurt us, we may not be able to trust others, including God. Or maybe a close friend or a spouse damaged our trust later in life. When someone who is important to us lets us down, we learn to distrust others. We find it hard to trust even God. We are constantly on guard, trying to protect ourselves against hurt.

Jonah is a good example of someone in the Bible who found it hard to trust God. We don't know what experiences in Jonah's life had made him that way; all we know is that when God told Jonah to go preach to the city of Nineveh, he refused. He didn't trust God to know what was best. Instead of having confidence in the goodness of God at work in the world, Jonah trusted only his own judgment. So he ran away from God.

We know what happened next to Jonah. He ended up in the belly of a great fish, all because he couldn't trust God. But God didn't abandon Jonah. Even in the dark, confined space within the fish, He was with Jonah—and He gave him a second chance.

Our lack of trust may have consequences, just as Jonah's did. But God doesn't get mad at us or punish us. He's right there with us in those consequences. He gives us another chance. He's so good to us!

LORD, WHEN I'M IN THE "BELLY OF THE WHALE," REMIND ME THAT YOU ARE THERE WITH ME. GIVE ME ANOTHER CHANCE TO BE A VEHICLE OF YOUR GOODNESS.

WHEN THE DOOR WON'T OPEN

"Ask and it will be given to you; seek and you will find; knock and the door will be opened to you."

MATTHEW 7:7 NIV

It's easy to believe Jesus' promises when things are going our way. When our families are happy and healthy, our finances stable, our jobs secure and fulfilling, we may *feel* blessed. We feel as though God has guided us to this place in our lives; He has kept His promises to us, and we praise Him.

But when everything seems to be falling apart and we can't see the answers to all the problems confronting us, we don't feel blessed at all. Sometimes it seems as though we've been knocking and knocking and knocking—and nothing in our lives is opening. Instead, everywhere we turn, we see only closed doors. We've been asking God—begging, pleading—but we see no answers. Our lives feel empty. We feel trapped by circumstances.

And yet Jesus says to us, "Don't be unsettled in your heart. Don't feel anxious and upset. You can believe Me. You can have confidence in the things I tell you. Trust me" (John 14:1, paraphrase).

Trusting when we can't see what God's doing is hard. But that's what trust is all about. The word *trust* comes from a very ancient root word that meant literally "firm, solid"—and trust requires that we walk out onto God's promises, believing that they are the most solid ground we will ever find upon which to build our lives.

If Jesus said we would be answered, then we need to keep asking, no matter how hoarse our voices have grown. If He said we would find what we're looking for, then we need to keep looking, even if we're exhausted from the search. And if He promised the door would be answered, then we need to continue to knock. We need to stake our lives on His promises.

"Trust in the LORD with all your heart and lean not on your own understanding" (Proverbs 3:5 NIV). Lean on God's promises instead.

....
....
....
....
....
....
....
....
....
....
....
....
....
....
....
....
....
....
....

GOD, I DON'T ALWAYS UNDERSTAND WHY YOU ALLOW EVENTS TO UNFOLD THE WAY THEY
DO. I DON'T HEAR WHAT YOU'RE SAYING TO ME, I CAN'T FEEL YOUR PRESENCE,
AND I CAN'T SEE ANY OPEN DOORS. BUT I STILL CHOOSE TO TRUST YOU.

TRANSFORMED CIRCUMSTANCES

Are any of you suffering hardships? You should pray.

JAMES 5:13 NLT

Prayer doesn't miraculously take away life's challenges. It's not a magic spell that makes all our troubles go *poof!* Jesus Himself prayed to be delivered from the cross—and yet He went to the cross and died there. The apostle Paul prayed to be delivered from "his thorn of the flesh"—but that didn't happen either.

You may think, *If God didn't answer even Jesus' and Paul's prayers the way they wanted, what's the point of me even trying?* But both Jesus and Paul show us how prayer changed them on the inside, allowing God to use their outer circumstances for His glory.

"My Father," Jesus prayed in the Garden of Gethsemane, "if it is not possible for this cup to be taken away unless I drink it, may your will be done" (Matthew 26:42 NIV). And Paul described his experience like this:

> *I was given the gift of a handicap to keep me in constant touch with my limitations. . . . At first I didn't think of it as a gift, and begged God to remove it. Three times I did that, and then he told me, "My grace is enough; it's all you need. My strength comes into its own in your weakness." Once I heard that. . .I quit focusing on the handicap and began appreciating the gift. It was a case of Christ's strength moving in on my weakness. Now I take limitations in stride, and with good cheer, these limitations that cut me down to size—abuse, accidents, opposition, bad breaks. I just let Christ take over!* (2 Corinthians 12:8–10 MSG)

We can see that prayer was the way both Jesus and Paul struggled with their emotional reactions to life's difficulties—and then, through prayer, they were able to accept God's will for their lives. Even more, their prayer gave God room to transform the meaning of their circumstances, so that pain and hardship became an opportunity for God's creative work.

Prayer can do the same for us. As it opens us up to God's Spirit, we will see Him working through us and in us, even in the midst of the most difficult times.

....
....
....
....
....
....
....
....
....
....
....
....
....
....
....
....
....
....

HELP ME, LORD, TO PRAY WITH PAUL AND JESUS: NOT MY WILL BUT YOURS BE
DONE IN MY LIFE. USE MY CIRCUMSTANCES IN WHATEVER WAY YOU WANT.

SUNSHINE IN THE DARK

Light is sweet; how pleasant to see a new day dawning.
ECCLESIASTES 11:7 NLT

Sometimes it seems that our lives are nothing but gray days. From small frustrations to major crises, life can be so hard. We get so used to clouds and gloom that sunshine seems like something we'll never experience again. With all the responsibilities and troubles in our lives, we may feel as though we'd be immature and shallow to even dream of sunny days. Sunshine is for kids, we think; grown-up life is serious.

God is there with us in our shadows, of course—but He also made the sunshine, and He wants to share it with us. He wants us to remember that even the longest nights come to an end, and the dreariest, darkest winters yield to spring. And He longs for us to see the ordinary wonder of each new sunrise.

We miss out on so many of the beauties God has sprinkled through our lives. We sit inside our dark houses, brooding over our troubles, so busy that we don't see the beam of sunlight that finds its way through a window. If we look outside, we may be surprised to find the sun is actually shining after all.

Every now and then, we need to remind ourselves to take a break from our lives' heavy loads. We need to make time for sunshine. If we take a moment to watch the dawn, the rest of our day will often go a little better. If we pause to feel the sun's warmth on our faces when we step outside, we may find ourselves soaking up a new sense of well-being. We may even find ourselves laughing more often.

Don't be so busy and grown up that you miss out on each day's light. The sunny side of life is every bit as real and valuable as life's gray days. Our God has things to share with you in the sunshine. He likes to see you smile. He loves to watch you play. He longs to hear you laugh. He wants you to know the reality of His joy and taste the delight of His presence.

GOD OF LIGHT, REMIND ME TODAY TO SEE THE SUNSHINE.
MAY I SMILE MORE, PLAY MORE, LAUGH MORE, DELIGHTING IN YOU.

WORSHIP AND HEALTH

Worship the LORD your God, and. . .
I will take away sickness from among you.

EXODUS 23:25 NIV

The word *worship* is one we often connect with going to church. We may think of singing praise songs or lifting our hearts in silent adoration to God. Those activities can all be aspects of worship. Some days, though, we just don't feel like singing choruses. Our lives are too busy for us to find quiet moments of adoration. We postpone worship for Sundays. God, however, wants worship to be a daily and constant part of our lives. Our very health depends on it!

The Old English word for worship points us in a slightly different direction from the way we usually think about worship, offering us a new perspective. "Worth-ship" was the English word used a thousand-some years ago, and it was based on a two-way relationship between a lord and his servant. The servant's "worth-ship" of the lord gave worth—valor, strength, and value—to the servant as well as the lord, for the two were linked together in a mutual commitment of honor and esteem.

Worship from this perspective is simply the daily living out of a mutual commitment. We can express that commitment in all sorts of ways—from praise choruses to vocal prayer to total silence—but ultimately, it is simply the relationship itself that creates this two-way stream of love and honor. When we enter into this relationship with the Lord of the universe, we receive infinite, eternal value and strength. We become whole, the people God created us to be.

The Bible clearly connects worship—a right relationship with God—with health and well-being. "If you will listen carefully to the voice of the LORD," God told Moses, "and do what is right in his sight, obeying his commands and keeping all his decrees," you will be healthy, not diseased, "for I am the LORD who heals you" (Exodus 15:26 NLT). Even if our bodies are sick, through worship we can experience inner health and wholeness.

SOMETHING NEW

And we know that in all things God works for the good of those who love him, who have been called according to his purpose.

ROMANS 8:28 NIV

When catastrophe strikes our lives, we're suddenly aware of how fragile our lives really are. There we were, going along with our normal routine, when without warning something bad happened. Our sense of safety and security is shattered. Life feels shaky, as though unexpected danger is lurking around every corner. It's hard to regain a sense of peace.

But God's love is powerful and creative. The same amazing divine energy that made the world is still at work in each and every circumstance of our lives. Even the most horrifying events can somehow be swept up by His power and made into something new, something that ultimately, in some way we probably can't even imagine now, will bless us and those we love.

True faith in God doesn't mean that we believe nothing bad will ever happen to us. Instead, it means we trust God to use even the bad things for our good and His glory. The book of Ecclesiastes tells us, "There is a time for everything, and a season for every activity under the heavens" (3:1 NIV). From God's perspective, there are no accidents. He never gets the timing wrong, and all His works are perfect. He knows what He's doing!

The psalmist wrote, "You go before me and follow me" (139:5 NLT). In other words, God knows what will happen to us in the future—and He's already there, in the midst of every circumstance. We can find Him in the catastrophes of life, waiting for us. He has a plan that He's unfolding for us even then.

"For I know the plans I have for you," God says to us. "They are plans for good and not for disaster, to give you a future and a hope" (Jeremiah 29:11 NLT). We can trust God even now—"for I am about to do something new," He tells us. "See, I have already begun! Do you not see it? I will make a pathway through the wilderness. I will create rivers in the dry wasteland" (Isaiah 43:19 NLT).

LOVING GOD, YOU ARE ALL-SEEING, ALL-KNOWING, ALL-POWERFUL, ALL-LOVING. IN YOU
THERE ARE NO ACCIDENTS, AND NO CATASTROPHE IS TOO BIG FOR YOU TO USE.
HELP ME TO TRUST YOUR PROMISES. DO SOMETHING NEW IN MY LIFE!

SMILE!

This is the day which the LORD hath made;
we will rejoice and be glad in it.

PSALM 118:24 KJV

Sometimes we act as though we think the Christian life was intended to be a serious, somber affair. We sigh and complain; we beg God to help us; and all the while, we're so focused on life's sadness and sorrow that we can't see the blessings that God has given, even in the midst of all our problems. God wants us to be glad!

The Bible is full of happy words: *gladness*, *pleasure*, *song*, *praise*, *joy*, and *rejoice*. Nowhere does it tell us, "Frown a lot. Sigh. Disapprove of people. Worry about things. Be sad. Think about nothing but sin and death and disappointment." And yet we don't take seriously the scripture's commandments to be joyful. We often don't even understand what they really mean.

The Bible's joy is always connected to the presence of God. It is the natural state in which we find ourselves if we walk with Him. It is the organic by-product of worship, our ongoing relationship with God. Worship and joy just naturally go together—and yet the grown-up world often tells us that taking time for pleasure, laughter, and play is irresponsible. It insists that we have to be productive in some way, every minute that we're awake.

With so much we're responsible for, so much we have to accomplish each and every day, we often don't have time for the sort of joy that children take for granted. Our sense of humor gets rusty, and we forget how to play. Everywhere we look, we see only shades of gray.

Life doesn't have to be like that. We can choose to live our lives differently. As Christ's followers, we can take time to laugh, to play, to rejoice in all God has given us. When we make this daily worship the "serious" focus of our daily lives, how can we help but sing with joy. . .leap with gladness. . .and rejoice in each and every day?

....
....
....
....
....
....
....
....
....
....
....
....
....
....
....
....
....
....

LORD, TODAY AS I GO ABOUT MY BUSINESS, REMIND ME TO SMILE. PUT SONGS IN
MY HEAD AND A SMILE ON MY LIPS. NUDGE ME WHENEVER YOU SEE
ME FORGETTING TO REJOICE IN THE DAY YOU GAVE ME.

COOL YOUR PIPES!

Bridle your anger, trash your wrath,
cool your pipes—it only makes things worse.

PSALM 37:8 MSG

When we're angry, it's hard to see God's blessings in our lives. Our anger can come between ourselves and God. It can cloud our vision, so that we can no longer see His goodness at work in our lives.

And yet when life doesn't go the way we want, it's so easy to feel angry. *I deserve better than this,* we may think. *This isn't fair. They shouldn't act that way. I shouldn't be treated like that. I shouldn't have to put up with this.* The more we think about it, the angrier we feel.

We all feel like this sometimes. But the Bible tells us to not nurse our anger. Instead of dwelling on it, the psalmist says that we should turn our backs on it. Instead of giving it room to run away with us, we are to bridle it.

Anger in and of itself is normal and can even be healthy. After all, Jesus got angry too! So we don't need to feel guilty for being angry. It's what we do with that anger that can be either healthy or harmful. When we let it eat way at our insides, a slow, burning resentment that corrodes our hearts, it damages our own inner selves—and when our anger drives our actions, when we lose control of ourselves because we're so full of rage, then we're likely to hurt those around us.

If we pay attention, we may notice that what angers us the most is often when we don't get our own way. We want to be in control of our lives. When we're not, even little things—a flat tire, a cracked dish, or even a broken fingernail!—can seem like the end of the world. No wonder then that bigger things— rebellious teenagers in the family, coworkers who get the promotions we'd hoped for, or chronic illnesses that get in the way of the lives we want for ourselves—can overwhelm us and rob us of the joy God wants us to know.

....
....
....
....
....
....
....
....
....
....
....
....
....
....
....
....
....

GOD, WHEN I'M ANGRY WITH THE WORLD, I ASK THAT YOU WOULD BE THE CONTAINER THAT HOLDS
MY TEMPER AND KEEPS IT FROM HURTING MYSELF AND OTHERS. I KNOW YOU ARE IN CONTROL.

ARGUMENTS

*We faced conflict from every direction,
with battles on the outside and fear on the inside.*
2 CORINTHIANS 7:5 NLT

Conflicts with others can absorb our attention. Whether it's an argument with our husband, a disagreement with a supervisor at work, or a misunderstanding with a friend, conflict can loom so large in our thoughts that we lose sight of God's presence. It's hard to feel like God is good when we're *so mad*! And as the apostle Paul understood, those external arguments bring internal anxiety to our hearts.

People in New Testament times had the same problem. The apostle James understood what was happening. "What causes fights and quarrels among you?" he wrote in his epistle. "Don't they come from your desires that battle within you? You desire but do not have, so you kill. You covet but you cannot get what you want, so you quarrel and fight. You do not have because you do not ask God. When you ask, you do not receive, because you ask with wrong motives, that you may spend what you get on your pleasures" (4:1–3 NIV). In other words, it's our selfishness that's causing so much anger and conflict in our lives.

James has some more words of advice when it comes to anger: "Everyone should be quick to listen, slow to speak and slow to become angry, because human anger does not produce the righteousness that God desires" (1:19–20 NIV). The sort of anger that springs from our selfishness keeps us from being the people God wants us to be—but if we turn outward, truly listening to those around us instead of focusing on what we think is best for our own selves, God can do amazing things.

The apostle Paul also gives us wise counsel when it comes to anger. "Make a clean break with all cutting, backbiting, profane talk," he wrote to the Ephesians. "Be gentle with one another, sensitive. Forgive one another as quickly and thoroughly as God in Christ forgave you" (4:31–32 MSG).

Notice that all these verses ask that we take responsibility for the conflicts in our lives. We like to blame the other party. We think to ourselves, *It's her fault we argued!* Or we tell ourselves, *He's to blame for this conflict, not me, so he's the one who needs to say he's sorry—not me!* The Bible, however, says nothing about the other person. Instead, it says, "Fools vent their anger, but the wise quietly hold it back" (Proverbs 29:11 NLT).

GIVE ME THE SELF-DISCIPLINE, LORD, TO CONTAIN MY ANGER. REMIND ME NOT TO
VENT MY FRUSTRATIONS ON OTHERS. RESTORE PEACE AND CALM TO MY HEART.

ANXIETY

*Banish anxiety from your heart and
cast off the troubles of your body.*
ECCLESIASTES 11:10 NIV

Sometimes anxiety seems like our hearts' default emotion. Are our loved ones safe? Will we do a good job on a challenging responsibility we've been given? Might that nagging pain be a symptom of a dangerous illness? Will people accept us? Will we be able to get everything done that needs doing? Will the people we love most make wise decisions? Do we have the right clothes for an upcoming event? Everywhere our thoughts turn, they encounter a new worry.

Psychological research has found that the cost of anxiety is high. It uses up energy that could be spent far more productively. It takes its toll on our bodies, giving us headaches and stomach problems. Even our immune systems suffer, making us more susceptible to colds and other illnesses. After long enough—when anxiety has become a way of life—it can even contribute to heart disease and high blood pressure. "Can all your worries add a single moment to your life?" Jesus asked during His Sermon on the Mount (Matthew 6:27 NLT). In fact, anxiety can actually shorten our lives! At the very least, worrying about the future—focusing on things that may never actually happen—robs us of the present moment's joy.

When Paul encountered this problem in the Philippian church, he gave them this advice: "Don't fret or worry. Instead of worrying, pray. Let petitions and praises shape your worries into prayers, letting God know your concerns. Before you know it, a sense of God's wholeness, everything coming together for good, will come and settle you down. It's wonderful what happens when Christ displaces worry at the center of your life" (Philippians 4:6–7 MSG).

When we catch ourselves brooding over our worries, we need to transform our anxiety into prayer. Each time we find ourselves fretting over what will happen regarding some situation, we can turn over that specific set of circumstances to God. As we make this practice a habit, we will find our trust in God is growing. Our anxiety will be replaced with God's peace.

....
....
....
....
....
....
....
....
....
....
....
....
....
....

LORD, I DON'T WANT TO PAY THE COST OF ANXIETY ANY LONGER. TAKE MY
WORRIES FROM ME, AND REPLACE THEM WITH PRAYER. FILL ME WITH
THE AWARENESS OF YOUR GOODNESS AT WORK IN MY LIFE.

THE ANXIETY ANTIDOTE

Love never gives up.
1 CORINTHIANS 13:7 MSG

When life seems bleak and we start doubting God's goodness, anxiety can spread like poison through our hearts. But there's an antidote for that poison. It's called "love."

Love may be a spiritual quality—but it's also as down-to-earth and practical as the air we breathe. As human beings, love is one of our most basic requirements. In fact, scientists tell us that love is as necessary to our lives as oxygen; babies, and even animals, need love to thrive. Psychologists also tell us that the more connected we are to others and to God, the healthier we will be, both physically and emotionally—and the less connected we are, the more we are at risk.

Our culture tends to believe that love "just happens." If we feel lonely and unloved, then we may assume we are just one of the unlucky people in the world who doesn't have enough love. But love doesn't work that way. Psychologist Erich Fromm called love "an act of will." To feel love in our lives, we have to make up our minds to act in loving ways. We have to put our love for God and others into practice.

God's love is never ending. There is nothing we need to do to deserve that love or to draw it to us. But there are practical ways that we can allow that love to flow through us to the world around us. Here are some of them:

- Focus on God and others. This means, don't obsess about your own concerns. Instead, shift your attention outside yourself. Spend time thinking about God. Notice the person next to you (whether that's your husband, a friend, a coworker, or a stranger you've met in passing).
- Practice looking at things from new perspectives. Consider others' points of view. Put yourself in their shoes, and take time to truly listen when they speak. Allow yourself to absorb God's perspective through scripture and prayer.
- Go out of your way to help someone else. Notice the needs around you—and do something practical to meet them, even in the smallest of ways.

"Love. . .puts up with anything. . .keeps going to the end" (1 Corinthians 13:7 MSG). It's an antidote to despair that never gives up.

THANK YOU, GOD OF LOVE, THAT YOUR LOVE FOR ME NEVER FAILS. PLEASE FILL ME UP WITH THAT LOVE, SO THAT THERE'S NO ROOM IN ME FOR ANXIETY, DOUBT, AND DESPAIR. MAKE ME A VEHICLE OF YOUR LOVE.

FINANCIAL WORRIES

If you. . .know how to give good gifts to your children, how much more will your Father in heaven give good gifts to those who ask him!
MATTHEW 7:11 NIV

One of the anxieties that is most likely to rob us of our confidence in God's goodness is worry about money. No matter how much money we have or don't have, most of us have lain awake at one time or another fretting over an overdue bill, an upcoming large expense, or the fear that our checking account will bounce before the next paycheck arrives.

Jesus' disciples also had financial responsibilities to meet. We may imagine them following Jesus without any practical concerns to hold them back—but although Jesus spoke often about the Kingdom of Heaven, He also made clear that His followers were to experience that Kingdom while still living here on earth. This meant someone had to pay for the food they ate, and someone had to pay the taxes. What's more, most of the disciples had families that needed their support.

To meet these financial needs, the disciples went fishing. John tells about one occasion like this in his Gospel. The men fished all night without catching anything. By morning, their hearts must have been heavy; no fish meant no money.

And then, Jesus called to them from the shore, " 'Fellows, have you caught any fish?' 'No,' they replied.

Then he said, 'Throw out your net on the right-hand side of the boat, and you'll get some!' So they did, and then they couldn't haul in the net because there were so many fish in it" (John 21:4–6 NLT).

Jesus knew how to supply the disciples' practical needs as well as their spiritual ones. God knows how to meet our needs too. He knows where to find the "fish" in our lives.

In Matthew 6:33, Jesus gave us the secret to having our financial needs met with this reminder: "If God gives such attention to the appearance of wildflowers—most of which are never even seen—don't you think he'll attend to you, take pride in you, do his best for you? What I'm trying to do here is to get you to relax, to not be so preoccupied with *getting*, so you can respond to God's *giving*. People who don't know God and the way he works fuss over these things, but you know both God and how he works. Steep your life in God-reality, God-initiative, God-provisions. Don't worry about missing out. You'll find all your everyday human concerns will be met" (Matthew 6:30–33 MSG).

GOD'S LONG ARM AND MIGHTY HAND

Remember that you were slaves in Egypt and that the LORD your God brought you out of there with a mighty hand and an outstretched arm.
DEUTERONOMY 5:15 NIV

Sometimes God can seem so very far away. When that happens, it's usually because we're focusing on the circumstances of our lives—and as a result, they loom so large that they block our vision of everything else, including God. When that happens, it's time to step back and get a new perspective.

Over and over in the Bible we read about God's long arm and strong hand. "You scattered Your enemies with Your mighty arm" (Psalm 89:10 NASB). "He hath done marvellous things: his right hand, and his holy arm, hath gotten him the victory" (Psalm 98:1 KJV). "He displayed his mighty power with his arm" (Luke 1:51 ISV). "They did not conquer the land with their swords; it was not their own strong arm that gave them victory. It was your right hand and strong arm and the blinding light from your face that helped them, for you loved them" (Psalm 44:3 NLT).

None of us can truly wrap our minds around divine power, but the Bible uses the metaphors of God's long arm and mighty hand to help us catch a glimpse of God's omnipotence. Whether it was to free the Israelites from slavery or redeem them from some foreign oppressor, God was never too far away to reach out on His people's behalf. And no matter how overwhelming the circumstances of our lives, His arm is long enough to reach us, and His hand is strong enough to help. When God seems far away from the troubles in our lives, the prophet Isaiah assures us, "The arm of the LORD is not too short to save" (59:1 NIV). No doubt or despair of ours can limit God's reach; no anxiety or fear can weaken His hand.

"Ah, Sovereign LORD, you have made the heavens and the earth by your great power and outstretched arm," said Jeremiah (32:17 NIV). The Creator of the universe is reaching into our lives with limitless power!

WHEN PEOPLE LET US DOWN

It is not an enemy who taunts me—I could bear that. It is not my foes who so arrogantly insult me—I could have hidden from them. Instead, it is you—my equal, my companion and close friend.

PSALM 55:12-14 NLT

At one time or another, most of us have felt that someone close to us has let us down. Often it's unintentional: our husbands are preoccupied and snap at us; a friend's careless comment hurts our feelings; or a coworker forgets to keep a promise. Things like that hurt badly enough, but it's even worse when someone we trusted purposefully stabs us in the back. That hurt can be overwhelming. It can come between our hearts and God and make us doubt even His goodness.

Christ too knew what it was like to be betrayed by a friend, both intentionally and unintentionally. He must have felt hurt when His friends were too tired to stay awake with Him during His spiritual battle in the Garden of Gethsemane on the night before His death. How much worse must have been the blow He felt when Judas betrayed Him with a kiss! And yet the Gospels give us no indication that He dwelt on these hurts or brooded over them. His love overcame the emotional pain He experienced and kept His course steady, allowing Him to lay down His life on behalf of both His friends and His enemies.

Following Jesus' example isn't easy. A first step could be to join the psalmist in this prayer:

Listen to me, God, and don't hide Yourself from me. Listen to me and answer me, even though my ears are filled with the voices of people who don't see my point of view. I feel oppressed by their opinions of me, and I am filled with restlessness and pain. They have a grudge against me, and now they're heaping trouble on me. They've let me down, and it hurts! It scares me too. But I'm calling on You, Lord, and I know You will rescue me. Morning, noon, and night—all day long, and all through the long, dark hours when I can't sleep—I will express all my feelings to You, because I know You're always listening. You will rescue me from all this trouble. Even though people have let me down, You will keep me safe. (Psalm 55, paraphrased)

FIERY FURNACES

Shadrach, Meshach, and Abednego replied, "O Nebuchadnezzar, we do not need to defend ourselves before you. If we are thrown into the blazing furnace, the God whom we serve is able to save us. He will rescue us from your power, Your Majesty. But even if he doesn't, we want to make it clear to you, Your Majesty, that we will never serve your gods or worship the gold statue you have set up."

DANIEL 3:16-18 NLT

The circumstances in Shadrach, Meshach, and Abednego's lives were probably worse than anything we've ever faced. The king wanted to control their lives, including their relationship with their God. When they refused to comply, he threw them into a furnace. If we were to find ourselves in that situation, we might easily feel that God had abandoned us. We might not see much evidence of His goodness!

But the three Israelite men were confident God would save them. They didn't know *how* God would accomplish their rescue—they were even able to accept that He might allow them to be burned to a crisp in Nebuchadnezzar's furnace—but they had no doubt that God's presence would be with them. They were right to trust God, because as things turned out, His presence with them was a literal fact. When the king looked into that blazing furnace, he saw not three men but four, and one of them "looked like a god" (Daniel 3:25). Ultimately, the three men emerged from the furnace unburned. God did indeed rescue them!

When we don't like what is happening in our lives, we have two choices: turn away from God and become bitter—or follow the example of Shadrach, Meshach, and Abednego and continue to rely on God, no matter what. If we take option one, ultimately we hurt ourselves more than we were already hurt. Bitterness robs us of joy and peace. The author of Hebrews tells us, "Keep a sharp eye out for weeds of bitter discontent. A thistle or two gone to seed can ruin a whole garden in no time" (12:15 msg). On the other hand, the second option—trusting God despite the difficult circumstances we face—can lead to a greater awareness of God's presence in our lives. The "fiery furnace" will still be there, burning as hot as ever—but we will find Jesus walking with us, in the midst of the flames.

"Be joyful in hope, patient in trouble, and persistent in prayer," Paul wrote to the Romans (12:12 isv). That's the formula for surviving life's fires!

DEAR GOD, HELP ME TO BE JOYFUL, PATIENT, AND PERSISTENT IN PRAYER—
EVEN WHEN MY LIFE IS LIKE A FURNACE I CAN'T ESCAPE. HELP ME
TO SEE YOUR SON WALKING BESIDE ME THROUGH THE FLAMES.

BATTLEFIELDS

When you go to war against your enemies and see horses and chariots and an army greater than yours, do not be afraid of them, because the LORD your God, who brought you up out of Egypt, will be with you. When you are about to go into battle, the priest shall come forward and address the army. He shall say: "Hear, Israel, today you are going into battle against your enemies. Do not be fainthearted or afraid; do not be terrified or give way to panic before them. For the LORD your God is the one who goes with you to fight for you against your enemies to give you victory."

DEUTERONOMY 20:1-4 NIV

Most of us aren't called to face actual warfare—but some days, the challenges in our lives can seem almost as threatening as a battlefield. We look at our lives, and our circumstances seem greater than we can handle. Our stomachs churn with anxiety whenever we think about the situation at work, our heads ache from the constant tension in our homes, and we wish we could just run away and hide somewhere no one would bother us. But we can't hide. We have to face the battles that lie ahead. These verses in Deuteronomy give us some good advice for dealing with moments like this.

First, instead of focusing on the enemy's "horses and chariots," remember all that God has done for us in the past. When we look back at other situations similar to the one we're facing now, we can see that God has never failed us. With hindsight, we can see how far God has brought us. . .and how many times He has saved us from situations that at the time seemed hopeless. Dwelling on God's goodness to us in the past helps us put the current situation in a new perspective. The army we're facing no longer looks so huge.

Second, we need to remind ourselves that God is the One who will fight the battle that lies ahead, not us. We don't have to stress out thinking about it. Instead, we place the entire situation in God's hands—and then we can relax, relying on Him for the victory.

HEAVENLY FRIEND, THE BATTLE AHEAD LOOKS TOO BIG FOR ME.
BUT I KNOW THAT WHEN I AM WEAK, YOU ARE STRONG. EASE MY
ANXIETY. KEEP ME FOCUSED ON YOUR GOODNESS AND POWER.

PRISON CELLS

By entering through faith into what God has always wanted to do for us—set us right with him, make us fit for him. . .we throw open our doors to God and discover at the same moment that he has already thrown open his door to us. We find ourselves standing where we always hoped we might stand—out in the wide open spaces of God's grace and glory.

ROMANS 5:1-2 MSG

"Now I want you to know, brothers and sisters, that what has happened to me has actually served to advance the gospel" (Philippians 1:12 NIV). When the apostle Paul wrote these words, he was referring to the fact that he was in prison. He wasn't there because he had committed any real crime but because he had offended the religious leaders of his day. When the Romans imprisoned him, they may have actually saved his life from the mob mentality that might have led to his death. Still, Paul was a captive. He wasn't free to come and go as he pleased.

Paul could easily have felt angry and frustrated; he could have despaired of ever being able to carry out the big plans he had for bringing the Good News of Jesus to the world. But instead, Paul wrote that his imprisonment was actually "advancing the gospel."

And he was right. His reputation as Christ's representative spread "throughout the whole praetorian guard," a body of ten thousand specially selected soldiers who were so powerful that even the emperors had to court their favor (Philippians 1:13). The apostle's influence spread beyond this elite group into the entire city; it even reached "Caesar's household" (Philippians 4:22). Because of Paul's example, many of the Roman Christians were "more abundantly bold to speak the word of God without fear" (Philippians 1:14).

Paul did not sulk and brood and feel resentful; he didn't lash out in bitterness against his captors. Instead, he remained cheerful. He made friends with his guards. And he knew God could use even his circumstances to create something good. What looked like restriction in his life was actually an open door that led to the Good News of Jesus spreading even further.

Do you ever feel like you too are in a prison cell of a sort? Loneliness can feel like a cell. So can illness and failure. When I feel trapped by these prison cells, I feel as though I'm stuck, unable to do the work I believe God has called me to do. But all the time, there's a doorway in every prison cell we encounter. And God is longing to send His creative goodness through that door, into our hearts and lives.

WHEN MY LIFE FEELS LIKE A PRISON CELL, LORD JESUS, SHOW ME THE DOORWAY THAT LEADS TO YOUR WILL FOR MY LIFE. BRING ME INTO THE "WIDE OPEN SPACES" OF YOUR GRACE AND GLORY, WHERE I'LL BE ABLE TO STAND TALL AND SHOUT YOUR PRAISE.

WALLS

It was by faith that the people of Israel marched around Jericho for seven days, and the walls came crashing down.

HEBREWS 11:30 NLT

Sometimes we build our own prison cells. When we can't see God's goodness, it could be because we've built walls around our hearts. We build those walls to protect our vulnerable hearts. We have been erecting these barriers all our lives, ever since as children we realized that the world was not the sunny, magical place we thought.

But walls not only keep things safe inside; they also can obstruct our view. These barricades may keep us from seeing how good God has been to us. They can trap us in a place where we are unable to experience the fullness of God's blessings. The walls that were meant to protect us can turn into a prison cell.

The psalmist David had an experience like this. He had taken refuge from his enemies in a cave—but now he realized that his safe place had turned into a prison. Lonely, scared, and overwhelmed, he wrote these words:

> *I look for someone to come and help me, but no one. . . cares a bit what happens to me. Then I pray to you, O LORD. I say, "You are my place of refuge. You are all I really want in life. Hear my cry, for I am very low. . . . Bring me out of prison so I can thank you. . . for you are good to me."* (Psalm 142:4–7 NLT)

David knew now that his attempts to find safety had been a waste of time and effort. All he really needed as his refuge was the presence of the Lord.

Think about it for a minute. What walls have you built between you and Jesus? What holds you captive, unable to experience the goodness of God at work in your life? Try making a list of each barrier you sense between you and God. Your list may be long—or it may have only one item, but that one item may loom tall and dark in your mind. Either way, Jesus came to earth as a human being to span all the barriers you've erected against His presence. His love is able to reach over the tallest wall.

Take the risk! Dare to be vulnerable. Trust Jesus.

KNOCK DOWN THE WALLS AROUND MY HEART, JESUS. SET ME FREE!

THE WALLS BETWEEN US

For he himself is our peace, who has made the two groups one and has destroyed the barrier, the dividing wall of hostility.

EPHESIANS 2:14 NIV

Some of the walls we build in life come between others and ourselves. They may be barriers of resentment we've erected against someone who hurt our feelings or treated us unfairly. They could be walls we've constructed against certain groups of people— perhaps those who don't share our politics or maybe people we believe threaten us in some way.

Whatever our reason for putting up these barricades between ourselves and others, we feel justified. *After all,* we tell ourselves, *it's their fault, not mine. I'm the innocent party here.* Or we may think to ourselves, *There's no point talking to people like that; they just don't listen.* We might tell ourselves, *Those people are dangerous, so I need to avoid them. To keep myself safe, I'm going to close my heart and mind to them.*

As time goes by, those walls rise even higher. We overlook the selfishness that lurks inside our hearts. We fail to see that what motivates us may be our need to have our own way, to think well of ourselves, or to be in control of the situation. So we focus on sealing up any cracks in their bricks. We make sure that our hearts and lives are safely protected from people we think might do us harm. It seems like the sensible thing to do.

But this isn't the way of Christ. When Jesus came to live with us as a human being, He made Himself vulnerable. And now, if we want to experience His grace and goodness in our lives, we have to be willing to let Him knock down all the "dividing walls of hostility" that we've built.

Jesus lives in our connections with others. He heals the breaks in our relationships; He knocks down the hostility inside our hearts, all those voices that insist on our own way, all the selfishness we feel, and all our need to be in control. When that happens, we may find we no longer look at others as threats to our well-being. The separations between us and others are bridged by Jesus. Now we can be truly one. Together, we can experience God's goodness.

....

....

....

....

....

....

....

....

....

....

....

....

....

....

....

....

DEAR JESUS, BE MY PEACE. UNITE ME ONCE MORE WITH THOSE
I HAVE SEPARATED MYSELF FROM. KNOCK DOWN THE WALLS.

GROW UP!

You're familiar with the old written law, "Love your friend," and its unwritten companion, "Hate your enemy." I'm challenging that. I'm telling you to love your enemies. Let them bring out the best in you, not the worst. When someone gives you a hard time, respond with the energies of prayer, for then you are working out of your true selves, your God-created selves. This is what God does. He gives his best—the sun to warm and the rain to nourish—to everyone, regardless. . . . In a word, what I'm saying is, Grow up. You're kingdom subjects. Now live like it. Live out your God- created identity. Live generously and graciously toward others, the way God lives toward you.

MATTHEW 5:43-48 MSG

We may consider ourselves to be faithful Christians—but do we take seriously what Jesus says here in the Gospel of Matthew? *I don't have any enemies,* we may think to ourselves. We forget about those people we've unfriended on Facebook because we didn't like their politics. . .and that group of people at church we ignore because they have different values from ours. . .and the woman in the neighborhood we avoid because she hurt our feelings once. . .and the administrators at work that we complain about constantly. We might deny that we treat any of these people like enemies—but do we act as though we love them? Do we give them our best? Do we pray for them with all our energy?

"Love your enemies!" Jesus told us emphatically. "Do good to them. . .without expecting to be repaid. Then your reward from heaven will be very great, and you will truly be acting as children of the Most High, for he is kind to those who are unthankful and wicked" (Luke 6:35 NLT). God is good to everyone, generous and kind even to those who reject Him.

If we want to really experience the goodness of God, we have to allow it to flow through us, out into the world, touching everyone in our lives, including our enemies: the people who have hurt us, the people we struggle to like, the people who disagree with us. And who knows? Those may be the very people through whom God is longing to demonstrate His goodness to us!

....
....
....
....
....
....
....
....
....
....
....
....
....
....
....
....

GOD OF LOVE, HELP ME TO GROW UP ENOUGH THAT I CAN LOVE MY ENEMIES.
USE ME TO REVEAL YOUR GOODNESS THROUGHOUT THE WORLD.

GARBAGE—OR COMPOST?

God is doing what is best for us, training us to live God's holy best. At the time, discipline isn't much fun. It always feels like it's going against the grain. Later, of course, it pays off handsomely, for it's the well-trained who find themselves mature in their relationship with God.

HEBREWS 12:10-11 MSG

"Why do you throw your garbage into a pile?" one of the children in my life asked me.

"Because," I said, "that garbage—all the eggshells and potato peelings and apple cores—will turn into dirt. And that dirt will make the tomato plants in our garden grow tall and healthy next summer."

"But it smells yucky."

"Yes, it does," I agreed. "But it's full of good stuff that will feed the garden."

Our lives are a little like that. What seems like garbage—a painful family history, an illness, a failure at work—can turn out to be something that helps us grow.

Author Alexander Solzhenitsyn spent ten long years in a Soviet work camp. In the midst of his captivity, he decided to find a new perspective, so that his suffering would serve some useful purpose. As a result, he was able to write later, after his release, "I nourished my soul there, and I say without hesitation: 'Bless you, prison, for having been in my life.' "[2] In the Old Testament, the prophet Isaiah also faced difficulty, but he too eventually saw a purpose in what he endured. "Surely," he said, "it was for my benefit that I suffered such anguish" (38:17 NIV).

Most of us will never have to face the sort of challenges Solzhenitsyn and Isaiah did—but we can cultivate a similar attitude as theirs. When our lives seem to pile up with garbage, we can choose to transform all that old, smelly stuff into compost.

When we do, the things in our life that seemed so worthless and painful can take on new meaning. We can begin to see the goodness of God, even in the midst of what we thought was trash. And He can use all of it—the entire stinky pile of rotten stuff—to help us become stronger and healthier, our roots deeper, our branches fuller.

---

[2] Alexander Solzhenitsyn, *The Gulag Archipelago: 1918-1956*, Volume 2, p. 617 (Toronto, ON: Harvill Press, 2003).

ILLNESS

Have compassion on me, LORD, for I am weak.
Heal me, LORD, for my bones are in agony.
PSALM 6:2 NLT

It's hard to see God's goodness when we're sick. Even an ordinary cold can cloud our perceptions—and when we face a more serious illness, we may be overwhelmed with an entire spectrum of emotions, from anger to despair, embarrassment to loneliness, fear to sorrow. We may feel it's just not fair, or we may want to give up. We feel frustrated we can't do all the things we normally do, and we may feel as though we're letting down our family, friends, and coworkers. We feel diminished, and we long to find the way back to our old healthy selves. At the same time, we may wish we never had to get out of bed. We're weak, exhausted, in pain. It's hard for us to interact with others the way we once did, and we may no longer enjoy the activities we once liked best. Even our spiritual lives suffer, and we feel guilty for not being more saintly. Life seems just too hard to face.

All these feelings are normal. They do not mean we are bad or weak, and they need not interfere with our relationships with God. They certainly won't prevent Him from showing us His goodness!

When Jesus was on earth, He healed all sorts of diseases. People were always reaching out to Him, clamoring for His healing. Just the touch of His robe sent His healing power flowing out to people who had been sick for years (Matthew 9:21). That power still exists in our world. Jesus still heals.

Sometimes, though, God asks us to bear our illnesses. Even then, however, He is bringing His healing, the deepest healing, the sort that reaches to the depths of our souls and lasts until eternity. "For I consider that the sufferings of this present time are not worthy to be compared with the glory that is to be revealed to us," wrote Paul (Romans 8:18 NASB).

....

....

....

....

....

....

....

....

....

....

....

....

....

....

....

....

....

HEALING LORD, USE ME, EVEN WHEN I'M SICK, TO REVEAL YOUR GLORY AND GOODNESS.

THE INVISIBLE WORLD

The Son is the image of the invisible God, the firstborn over all creation.
COLOSSIANS 1:15 NIV

We live in a time and place where science is valued. Science can show us many wonders, and it has made our lives easier and healthier in many ways. But with all our emphasis on science, we sometimes assume that everything in the universe can be measured and observed. We think that things that are invisible must also be imaginary. Even those of us who believe in God may keep our beliefs shut up in a little box that's separated from everything we know about the scientific world. But this is a simplistic worldview (one that's not even very scientific!) that overlooks the mystery of life. It denies us access to the invisible God who fills the visible world with His goodness.

Earlier cultures may have found it easier to believe in an invisible world, but like us, the heroes of the Old Testament had to choose whether to focus on the visible world or the invisible. The author of Hebrews tells us that "by faith Abraham, when called to go to a place he would later receive as his inheritance, obeyed and went, even though he did not know where he was going" (11:8 NIV). This chapter in the book of Hebrews talks about others as well as Abraham—Noah, Moses, Sarah, Joseph, Isaac, and Jacob—and then it goes on to say, "All these people. . .show that they are looking for a country of their own. If they had been thinking of the country they had left, they would have had opportunity to return. Instead, they were longing for a better country—a heavenly one" (vv. 13–16).

It's hard to believe in a better country that's not visible to us now. All sorts of everyday material things are all around us, and these things can very easily seem more real to us than God does. But Hebrews reminds us that Moses "persevered because he saw him who is invisible" (Hebrews 11:27 NIV). Obviously, Moses valued his spiritual vision as much as he did his physical eyesight. He took seriously the promise of an invisible country.

INVISIBLE GOD, BE MORE REAL TO ME THAN THE WORLD I CAN SEE AND TOUCH.
BRING ME TO YOUR COUNTRY, THE PLACE WHERE YOUR
GOODNESS IS ETERNALLY REVEALED.

THE KINGDOM OF GOD

Thy kingdom come, Thy will be done in earth, as it is in heaven.

MATTHEW 6:10 KJV

When Jesus was on earth, He spoke often about God's kingdom. He wasn't talking about heaven, though. Instead, He was referring to the realm where God's goodness has full sway, a realm that is already present, because Jesus brought to earth God's saving rule.

When we pray that God's kingdom come and His will be done, we are aligning ourselves with God's goodness in our individual lives, as well as in our world as a whole. We are accepting Christ's agenda as our own. Like Him, we will overflow with the "glad tidings of the kingdom of God" (Luke 8:1 KJV).

But we can't always see this reality. That's because, as Jesus reminded us, "The kingdom of God is not coming with a visible display" (Luke 17:20 ISV). Paul explained further, saying, "For the kingdom of God is not meat and drink; but righteousness, and peace, and joy in the Holy Ghost" (Romans 14:17 KJV).

Again and again throughout the Gospels, Jesus talks about the Kingdom of God, using simile after simile to help us grasp what He's trying to say. On one occasion, He told His followers, "The Kingdom of God is like a farmer who scatters seed on the ground" (Mark 4:26 NLT). What did He mean by that? Maybe that we can find God's goodness everywhere, scattered throughout our world by His generous hand.

Another time, Jesus said, "The kingdom of God. . .is like a grain of mustard seed, which, when it is sown in the earth, is less than all the seeds that be in the earth" (Mark 4:30–31 KJV). This simile tells us that sometimes we may be able to catch only the tiniest glimpse of God's Kingdom—and yet that tiny seed of divine goodness can grow and spread into our lives and out into the world.

These are just a few of the word pictures Jesus used to describe the kingdom. He also compared this realm to a treasure buried in a field. . .to a king preparing for a wedding feast . . .and to a little child. Ultimately, He reminded us that we can't point to this and that and say, "Look, there it is!"—"for, behold, the kingdom of God is within you" (Luke 17:21 KJV).

....
....
....
....
....
....
....
....
....
....
....
....
....
....
....
....
....
....

LORD, OPEN MY HEART SO THAT YOU CAN PLANT YOUR KINGDOM'S SEED IN ME.
MAY IT GROW WITHIN ME INTO A PLANT THAT'S STRONG AND TALL AND
HEALTHY. USE ME TO SPREAD YOUR GOODNESS THROUGH THE WORLD.

RESURRECTION

Jesus said. . . , "I am the resurrection and the life. The one who believes in me will live, even though they die."

JOHN 11:25 NIV

We can't escape the reality of death. Even in our twenty-first-century world, where our lifetimes are often extended by good medical care, sooner or later death catches up with each of us. In the meantime, beloved family members and friends leave this life ahead of us, breaking our hearts. Death is a dark shadow that lies over all the love and joy in our lives. We can pretend we don't see it, but one day death will bring an end to all we love so much in this world. How can God be good when every beautiful baby will one day have to face death?

As Christians, we say we believe in the resurrection of the dead, but deep in our hearts, we may have doubts. The closer death comes to us, the harder it may be for us to hold on to our confidence in eternal life. When death starts breathing down our necks—when a spouse or close friend dies, as we grow older, or if we are asked to face a serious illness—our doubts may become overwhelming. Is there really anything beyond death? Or will all that we are cease to exist once we stop breathing?

It is natural to fear death. Even Jesus, when He heard that His friend Lazarus had died, shed tears of sorrow. On the night before the Crucifixion, He had to struggle to accept the death that lay ahead of Him. So He understands our fears and doubts.

And He says to us, "Trust me. There is plenty of room for you in my Father's home. If that weren't so, would I have told you that I'm on my way to get a room ready for you? And if I'm on my way to get your room ready, I'll come back and get you so you can live where I live" (John 14:2–4 MSG).

The Bible assures us that physical death is not the end. Jesus came to this earth so that our fears could be put to rest. He has promised us that He has prepared a place for us in the life to come—and when we die, we will hear His voice welcoming us home. His goodness will last forever.

JESUS, YOU ARE MY RESURRECTION. YOU GIVE ME LIFE EVEN IN THE MIDST OF DEATH. HELP ME TO FOLLOW YOUR EXAMPLE ON THE CROSS AND COMMIT MY SPIRIT INTO GOD'S HANDS, TRUSTING THAT HIS GOODNESS WILL NEVER FAIL ME—EVEN AT MY DEATH.

HUMBLE PIE

Take my yoke upon you. Let me teach you, because I am humble and gentle at heart, and you will find rest for your souls.
MATTHEW 11:29 NLT

True humility, the sort that Jesus longs to teach us, is a vehicle for God's goodness. Strangely, though, our lack of humility may disguise itself as dissatisfaction with ourselves. We compare ourselves to others around us, and we find that we never seem to measure up. We wish we could accomplish as much as our sister seems to in a day, or that we could keep our homes as tidy as our neighbor does, or that our children would behave as well as our friends' children do. We wish we were smarter. . .prettier . . .more respected at work. . .a better cook. . .calmer. . .more talented. . .thinner. . .more creative.

And all the while, Jesus is longing for us to humbly reach out and take the gift of our own true selves. He wants us to accept the people we are—and then offer those people, with all their imperfections, back to Him. He wants us to be at rest, at peace with ourselves as we are.

Many times, though, our pride stands in Jesus' way. We long to be just a little bit (or a lot!) better than others. We want to impress people; we yearn to stand out from the crowd. Somehow, we manage to be unsure of our own worth—and totally self-preoccupied, all at the same time.

Jesus says to us, "Do you want to stand out? Then step down. Be a servant. If you puff yourself up, you'll get the wind knocked out of you. But if you're content to simply be yourself, your life will count for plenty" (Matthew 23:11–12 MSG). Only in Jesus can we realize the goodness of our own selves!

We often overlook the value of humility, but the Bible puts it in the same category with truth and justice. "In your majesty," wrote the psalmist, "ride out to victory, defending truth, humility, and justice. Go forth to perform awe-inspiring deeds!" (Psalm 45:4 NLT). Humility allows God to use us. It makes room for the victory of truth, justice, and goodness in our world.

GOD, I DON'T LIKE HAVING TO EAT HUMBLE PIE—BUT IF IT MAKES ME
MORE USEFUL TO YOU, THEN I'LL TAKE A SECOND HELPING!

GOD NEVER FORGETS

Zion said, The LORD hath forsaken me,
and my Lord hath forgotten me.
ISAIAH 49:14 KJV

Do you ever wonder if God has forgotten you? Sometimes He allows a long period of pain and hardship in our lives, and we begin to wonder if He really cares. *He must have given up on me,* we may think. *He doesn't really care about me. My life is too unimportant to concern the Creator of the universe. God may be good all the time—but His goodness doesn't do me any good!*

That's how the people of Israel were feeling when they ended up held captive in Babylon, far from their homeland. Thinking that they were forgotten and abandoned was the only way they knew to explain to themselves why God wasn't rescuing them the way they wanted. In a similar way, when we don't sense that God is present with us, and we don't see Him saving us from the crises in our lives, we assume He has forgotten us and given up on us. His goodness has its limits, we believe, because we don't see it reaching into our lives.

But in the same chapter of Isaiah, God answers His people:

> *When the time's ripe, I answer you.*
>   *When victory's due, I help you.*
> *I form you and use you*
>   *to reconnect the people with me,* . . .
> *Heavens, raise the roof! Earth, wake the dead!*
>   *Mountains, send up cheers!*
> *GOD has comforted his people.*
>   *He has tenderly nursed his beaten-up, beaten-down people.* . . .
> *"You'll know then that I am GOD.*
>   *No one who hopes in me ever regrets it."* . . .
> *"Even if. . .a tyrant holds my people prisoner,*
> *I'm the one who's on your side,*
>   *defending your cause, rescuing your children.* (Isaiah 49:8, 13, 23, 26 MSG)

God never forgets His people! When the time is ripe, His goodness bursts into bloom. No one who trusts Him will ever regret it.

THANK YOU, FAITHFUL LORD, FOR ANSWERING ME IN YOUR TIME. HELP ME TO WAIT
FOR YOU TO RESCUE ME, CONFIDENT THAT YOU'LL NEVER EVER FORGET ME.

HEAVY HEADS

*Thou, O LORD, art a shield for me; my glory,
and the lifter up of mine head.*

PSALM 3:3 KJV

Some mornings, it's hard just to lift our heads off our pillows. From the moment we wake up, we're already thinking, *If only I could stay in bed today. I just don't feel like facing the day.* We pull ourselves out from under the covers and stumble through our morning routines, but our heads feel heavy all day. We long to lay them down, just for a few moments, and rest. Our lives seem overwhelming.

When David wrote Psalm 3, he had good reason for feeling like that. His son Absalom was trying to kill him so he could become king in David's place, and David was on the run from his own son. Talk about a family conflict! The people around him weren't much help; "God will never rescue him," they were saying (v. 2). "It's no use, David. You might as well give up."

And at this moment, when David must have longed to crawl into a hole and never come out, he sat down and wrote a poem that affirmed his faith in God. He knew he could count on God's goodness—and he knew God would lift his heavy head and give him the energy he needed to face the immense challenges of his life.

David knew that human help was not enough. "From the Lord comes deliverance," he wrote (v. 8). As he woke up and faced the dangers of a new day, he wasn't relying on his own strength to get him through, nor did he count on his friends or his troops to give him protection. He knew that God would come to his rescue. He would save David from his enemies—and from his exhaustion and discouragement as well.

When our heads hang heavy, all we can see is the ground. God longs to lift our heads and give us a new perspective. When we look up, we'll see the sky—and we'll find His goodness shining on us.

SEXUAL DISCRIMINATION

God created human beings in his own image. In the image of God he created them; male and female he created them.

GENESIS 1:27 NLT

Our world today is filled with stories about women who have been treated unfairly by men. Some people even put the blame on Christianity for the inequality between the sexes. It's hard to have faith in a good God if we imagine Him as a domineering male who considers women to be inferior!

From the very beginning of the Bible, however, scripture indicates the value God puts on women. In a culture where women were often considered property, the Bible nevertheless makes clear the importance individual women have played in God's plan for the world. What's more, scripture tells us that humankind needs both genders to be complete. Together, males and females, we are the image of God. Our interactions as men and women are intended to be one way the goodness of God enters our world. But we live in a fallen world, and what was intended to be a vehicle of God's blessing has often been twisted or broken. When that happens, women often suffer.

The biblical accounts of male-female interactions indicate that when these go off course and become abusive or exploitive, the entire community suffers. The implication is that we cannot say these are private sins, between the injured party, God, and ourselves. When man-woman relationships are unhealthy, the entire community is affected. Healthy man-woman relationships, the Bible tells us, however, bless the entire community.

God designed us for relationships with each other, and men and women's interactions can lead to one of the deepest of all human relationships. Like the Song of Solomon's portrayal of intimate joy, the New Testament indicates that male-female interactions can also reveal to us the loving self-sacrifice of Christ's relationship with the Church. Through healthy, respectful relationships with the opposite sex, we can come to understand more deeply our relationship with God.

Ultimately, however, the Bible indicates that our gender is not what is most important in God's eyes. Galatians 3:28 (NIV) tells us that in Christ, "There is neither. . .male and female, for you are all one in Christ Jesus." In *The Message*, this verse reads: "Among us you are all equal. That is, we are all in a common relationship with Jesus Christ." Sexual discrimination goes against the goodness of God.

JESUS, THANK YOU FOR ALL THE WAYS YOU SHOWED YOUR RESPECT FOR WOMEN.
WHEN I FEEL ANGRY, AFRAID, OR INFERIOR—SIMPLY BECAUSE I'M A WOMAN—
REMIND ME THAT IN YOUR EYES I AM EQUAL AND IMPORTANT.

RACIAL PREJUDICE

*Many of the Samaritans believed in Him
because of the word of the woman.*

JOHN 4:39 NASB

The Jews of Jesus' day didn't like the Samaritans. They considered the people of Samaria to be "half-breeds," inferior people who didn't worship God correctly. If anyone had asked them, the Jews would probably have said that their prejudice was justified. The Jews were "good people" who worshipped the true God. In their minds, they weren't anything like those sinful Samaritans!

Few of us want to admit to being prejudiced against any race or ethnic group—and yet in today's world, there are groups of people we judge and fear and sometimes even hate. These people don't know God the way we do, and like the Jews, we think our opinions are justified. After all, we too are good people who worship the true God!

Thanks to the racial prejudice they encountered, the people of Samaria might have had negative feelings about the Jewish God. From their perspective, He would have looked cruel and uncaring, concerned only with His own people. Do people looking at us ever wonder about the God we serve? Judging by our actions, how good does our God look?

In the Gospel of John, Jesus shows us a different way. As He and His disciples travel from Judea to Galilee, they pass through Samaria and stop outside a village. Jews normally avoided contact with their Samaritan neighbors by traveling other, longer routes to avoid their lands, and the disciples probably felt about as comfortable as a group of white businessmen might feel today strolling through an all-black, inner-city neighborhood.

While the disciples go into town to buy food, Jesus stays behind and rests by Jacob's Well, an ancient holy site. When a Samaritan woman comes to the well to draw water, He initiates a conversation with her. Here, as so often in the Gospel accounts, Jesus does not treat people according to cultural expectations. He reaches out to the Samaritan woman and draws her into a relationship with Him. The woman then carries the news of Jesus back to her village, making her one of the first missionaries to carry the Gospel.

If a modern-day church was choosing the appropriate person to evangelize a new group, it's unlikely they would choose someone like the woman at the well—but Jesus looked past His culture and saw this woman as the ideal person to relay the Good News of God's love and goodness toward *all people.*

DEAR GOD, WHEN OTHERS LOOK AT ME, MAY THEY SEE
NOT MY PREJUDICE BUT YOUR GOODNESS.

OFF COURSE

He is so rich in kindness and grace that he purchased our freedom with the blood of his Son and forgave our sins.

EPHESIANS 1:7 NLT

Sin is serious. And yet the word Paul used in this verse, the word that's translated as "sin," actually meant a misstep, a slip-up. That doesn't sound as serious, does it? According to *HELPS Word Studies*, however, the literal meaning was "a falling away after being close-beside." In other words, sin is anything that interferes with our relationship with God. It's whatever comes between our hearts and Him. It is everything that makes us go off course, away from the path God wants for our lives.

Once we realize our mistakes, we may feel guilty and ashamed. We get discouraged with ourselves. But Jesus came to take away those feelings. He came to get us back on course. No matter how many times we swerve off track, He's always ready to reach out His hand and pull us back.

He tells us this is true again and again in the Gospels. "The Son of man hath power on earth to forgive sins," He said (Mark 2:10 KJV), and "There is forgiveness of sins for all who repent" (Luke 24:47 NLT). On the night before His death, at the Last Supper, He told His disciples, "This is my blood, which confirms the covenant between God and his people. It is poured out as a sacrifice to forgive the sins of many" (Matthew 26:28 NLT).

The rest of the Bible assures us of the same message. "When we were overwhelmed by sins, you forgave our transgressions," wrote the psalmist (65:3 NIV). "In your love you kept me from the pit of destruction," the prophet Isaiah said to God, "you have put all my sins behind your back" (Isaiah 38:17 NIV). And God told Isaiah, "I—yes, I alone—will blot out your sins for my own sake and will never think of them again" (43:25 NLT). The author of Hebrews has the same message for us from God: "I will be merciful to their unrighteousness, and their sins and their iniquities will I remember no more" (Hebrews 8:12 KJV). And finally, "He has removed our sins as far from us as the east is from the west" (Psalm 103:12 NLT).

FORGIVING LORD, REMIND ME THAT THE WORST THING ABOUT SIN IS
THAT IT SEPARATES ME FROM YOU. GET ME BACK ON COURSE, I PRAY.
RESTORE OUR RELATIONSHIP AND THROW MY SIN FAR, FAR AWAY.

DAILY BREAD

Give us today our daily bread.

MATTHEW 6:11 NIV

We often feel as though there's some sort of shortage in our lives. Even if we have enough "bread," we almost always feel we're lacking *something*. We might need more savings to finance our children's college education or our retirements. It could be we need a new, more reliable car. Or it could be something intangible we lack, such as patience, opportunities to be creative, or the emotional strength to cope. Often, the thing we feel we're most in need of is more time! We could consider any of these things to be the "bread" Jesus was talking about when He gave us the "Lord's Prayer." "Bread" could be any of the most basic things we need to live happy, healthy lives.

Notice that in Jesus' prayer, He doesn't mention a weekly, monthly, or yearly supply. Just as God sent the Israelites manna to collect each morning—food that spoiled when they tried to stockpile it for the next day—God promises to give us exactly what we need for the day ahead. Day by day, He meets our needs for physical and spiritual food.

"One day at a time," is one of the slogans that Alcoholics Anonymous teaches to its members. It's a principle that's also embedded in the prayer Jesus taught us. God wants us to depend on Him, each day of our lives, believing that He will give us exactly what we need. That's what it means to walk by faith.

When your faith wavers, reread the many promises in scripture about God's providence. Let them sink into your mind, replacing your anxiety. Here are just a few:

God will generously provide all you need. Then you will always have everything you need and plenty left over to share with others. (2 Corinthians 9:8 NLT)

My God shall supply all your need according to his riches in glory by Christ Jesus. (Philippians 4:19 KJV)

The LORD is my shepherd, I shall not want. (Psalm 23:1 KJV)

Consider the crows. They don't plant or harvest, they don't even have a storeroom or barn, yet God feeds them. How much more valuable are you than birds! (Luke 12:24 ISV)

....
....
....
....
....
....
....
....
....
....
....
....
....
....
....
....
....
....

THANK YOU, LOVING GOD, THAT YOU WILL GIVE ME EXACTLY WHAT I NEED TODAY.

STUMBLING IN THE DARK

Let the one who walks in the dark, who has no light,
trust in the name of the LORD and rely on their God.
ISAIAH 50:10 NIV

We somehow feel that things aren't right if we can't see where we're going. We seem to think that we *deserve* to know the road ahead. We feel as though we're more in control of life when we can see what lies up ahead.

But none of us can truly see the future—and none of us can control all aspects of our lives. That's where faith comes in.

Paul wrote, "This happened that we might not rely on ourselves but on God" (2 Corinthians 1:9 NIV). He knew that it doesn't take faith to walk confidently in the bright sunlight of noon. At times like that, we can rely on our own intelligence and abilities. Faith comes into play, however, when we walk forward through pitch darkness, relying totally on the grasp of God's hand on ours for guidance. It's what the Bible means when it says we are to "walk by faith and not by sight" (2 Corinthians 5:7).

But we like to try to figure out things for ourselves. We say, "Sure, this is a bad situation, but I think I can see what God is doing through all of this." We forget what the author of Proverbs wrote: "Trusting the LORD leads to prosperity. Those who trust their own insight are foolish" (28:25–26 NLT). And then, when we can't see any good that is being accomplished, though, when we're confused and uncertain, we have nothing left to do but to trust God.

And God is trustworthy! He brings good in ways we don't understand. Some other verses in Proverbs put it like this: "Trust GOD from the bottom of your heart; don't try to figure out everything on your own. Listen for GOD's voice in everything you do, everywhere you go; he's the one who will keep you on track. Don't assume that you know it all. Run to GOD! Run from evil! Your body will glow with health, your very bones will vibrate with life!" (3:5–8 MSG).

....
....
....
....
....
....
....
....
....
....
....
....
....
....
....
....
....
....

I CAN'T SEE THE PATH AHEAD, LORD—SO I'M PUTTING MY HAND IN YOURS. PLEASE SHOW ME
THE WAY TO GO. HELP ME TO WALK BY FAITH AND NOT BY SIGHT. I WANT TO
GLOW WITH YOUR GOODNESS AND VIBRATE WITH YOUR LIFE!

BAD NEWS

He will never be shaken; The righteous. . .will not fear evil tidings; His heart is steadfast, trusting in the LORD. His heart is upheld, he will not fear.

PSALM 112:6-8 NASB

When the phone rings in the middle of the night, it's never good news! Even if it turns out to be just a wrong number, we're left with our hearts pounding, adrenaline surging through us. Our bodies have kicked into their natural "fight-or-flight" reaction. Sleep is often a long time coming once that happens. We lie in bed, worrying about our friends and family. Are they safe in their beds? Or is one of our children out on the roads? Will a loved one's symptoms turn out to be serious? When we get the results from our mammogram, will we discover we have breast cancer? Our imaginations can run crazy while we lie there in the darkness.

But the Bible tells us we don't have to put ourselves through this. We don't need to be afraid of bad news. When we put our trust in God, our hearts will be steadfast, unshaken. Even when the bad news is real, not just a wrong number, God will hold us up.

Author Darlene Sala once wrote:

> *Bad news is like a storm that rises quickly on the ocean of our lives and would sink our ship if we didn't do something quickly. When the storm comes, we need a harbor where we can drop anchor. "I would hurry to my place of shelter, far from the tempest and storm" says the psalmist (55:8). A steadfast heart is simply one who has run to the Lord for shelter.[3]*

This is practical advice! It reminds us that when the phone rings in the night, our first action, before we even pick up the phone, should be to turn it over to God. He is our place of shelter, and He can hold us steady, no matter how bad the news turns out to be. His goodness never fails.

---

[3] Darlene Sala, *Inspiring Words for Women* (Uhrichsville, OH: Barbour Publishing, Inc., 2005).

I HAVE ANCHORED MY HEART IN YOU, LORD GOD. HOLD ME STEADY;
KEEP ME FROM FALLING, NO MATTER WHAT HAPPENS.

DEPRESSION

*The LORD is close to the brokenhearted
and saves those who are crushed in spirit.*

PSALM 34:18 NIV

According to psychologists, depression is far more than a sad feeling. It's an illness, as real as the flu, that causes a persistent feeling of sadness. Researchers have found that depression is the most common of all psychiatric disorders. Almost all of us, at one time or another in our lives, will experience it. When we do, we can't just "snap out of it."

When we're depressed, we lose interest in life. Depression affects how we feel, think, and behave, and it can lead to a variety of other emotional and physical problems. We may have trouble doing our normal day-to-day activities; we may even feel as if life isn't worth living. Depression is a deep-seated feeling that grabs hold of us and doesn't let go, day after day. It can take a toll on our social lives, our professional lives, our spiritual lives, and our physical health. Depression can cast a cloud over our hearts and minds. From within that cloud, nothing looks good—even God.

As Christians, we may feel we should be immune to depression. But depression is no sin! God has promised us He will be especially close to us when we go through these bleak times. He will be there at our side, waiting to lead us into His joy once more. With David, we can pray:

I'm waiting patiently for You, Lord. I know You will lean down to me and hear my cry. You will draw me up out of the pit of destruction, this miry bog of depression where I'm stuck. You will set my feet on the rock, and You will make my steps steady. And then You will put a new song in my mouth, a song of praise to God. Many will see what You have done for me, and they too will put their trust in You. (Psalm 40:1–3, paraphrased)

Lord, You reached down from above. You took and drew me up out of the deep waters of depression. You delivered me from my strong enemy, from this depression that was too strong for me to overcome on my own. When calamity seemed to surround me, You held me steady. You brought me forth into a large place, a place of freedom and emotional health. You delivered me. (2 Samuel 22:17–20, paraphrased)

....
....
....
....
....
....
....
....
....
....
....
....
....
....
....
....
....
....

I FEEL CRUSHED, LORD. DEPRESSION CASTS ITS SHADOW OVER MY ENTIRE LIFE.
I CAN'T FEEL YOU WITH ME—BUT I TRUST YOU ARE THERE, CLOSE BESIDE ME.

HOPE

May the God of hope fill you with all joy and peace as you trust in him, so that you may overflow with hope by the power of the Holy Spirit.
ROMANS 15:13 NIV

"We must accept finite disappointment," Martin Luther King Jr. said once, "but we must never lose infinite hope." He went on to say, "Everything that is done in the world is done by hope." Dr. King understood that hope plays an essential role in our lives. In the midst of disappointments, hope is what gives us the energy to keep going, working for a better future.

This kind of hope isn't a cheery outlook, and it isn't the same as *wanting* something to happen. Instead, it's a confidence that good things will come to fruition in the future. The ancient word root for "hope" was related to "hop," indicating that hope is active. It propels us forward into the future. Hope leaps across the gap between things as they are now and things as they will be one day.

Take a moment to think about these quotations about hope:

Hope begins in the dark, the stubborn hope that if you just show up and try to do the right thing, the dawn will come. You wait and watch and work: you don't give up. (Anne Lamot)

When you say a situation or a person is hopeless, you're slamming the door in the face of God. (Charles L. Allen)

Hope is always available to us. When we feel defeated, we need only take a deep breath and say, "Yes," and hope will reappear. (Monroe Forester)

The Bible also has a lot to say about hope. The verse above from Romans tells us that God is a God of hope. Hope is part of His nature. Because of God's goodness, we have hope in this world, as well as hope for eternity. "Rejoice in our confident hope," Paul wrote later in his letter to the Romans (12:12 NLT). How do we do that? In the same verse, Paul gives us the formula: "Be patient in trouble, and keep on praying."

GOD OF HOPE, HELP ME TO BE PATIENT IN THE MIDST OF TROUBLE, AND TO TURN TO
YOU ALWAYS IN PRAYER, SO THAT I CAN BE FILLED WITH YOUR HOLY CONFIDENCE.

SURRENDER

O people of Judah and Jerusalem, surrender your pride and power.
Change your hearts before the LORD.
JEREMIAH 4:4 NLT

The Old Testament tells the story of Ben-hadad, the king of Syria who defeated Ahab, the king of Israel. When Ahab surrendered, he told the Syrian king, "I am thine, and all that I have" (1 Kings 20:4 KJV). That is what it also means to surrender to God: to tell Him, "I am Yours and so is everything I have." When we look at our lives and fail to see God's goodness, it may be because we have failed to truly surrender ourselves to Him. Author Andrew Murray had this to say about the connection between surrender and the goodness of God:

> Who is God? He is the Fountain of life, the only Source of existence and power and goodness, and throughout the universe there is nothing good but what God works. God has created the sun, and the moon, and the stars, and the flowers, and the trees, and the grass; and are they not all absolutely surrendered to God? Do they not allow God to work in them just what He pleases? When God clothes the lily with its beauty, is it not yielded up, surrendered, given over to God as He works in its beauty?
>
> . . .God is life, and love, and blessing, and power, and infinite beauty, and God delights to communicate Himself to every child who is prepared to receive Him; but ah! this one lack of absolute surrender is just the thing that hinders God.[4]

Murray goes on to say,

> You know in daily life what absolute surrender is. You know that everything has to be given up to its special, definite object and service. I have a pen in my pocket, and that pen is absolutely surrendered to the one work of writing, and that pen must be absolutely surrendered to my hand if I am to write properly with it. If another holds it partly, I cannot write properly.

Surrender is not the negative thing we often imagine it to be. Instead, it allows us to become the people God intended us to be, functioning fully as our true selves, living lives filled to the brim with the goodness of God.

---

[4] Andrew Murray, *Absolute Surrender: The Blessedness of Forsaking All and Following Christ* (Radford, VA: Wilder Publications, 2009).

GOD, POINT OUT ANYTHING I'M HOLDING BACK FROM YOU. HELP ME TO
SURRENDER EVERYTHING I AM AND EVERYTHING I HAVE TO YOU.

123

COFFEE CUPS

Blessed is the one who comes in the name of the LORD.
PSALM 118:26 NASB

God longs to bless us with goodness in every facet of our lives. But sometimes we get in His way.

Think about a coffee cup sitting on the kitchen counter, clean and empty, just waiting for you to pour your morning brew into it. That's how we need to come to God—open and ready to receive what He wants to pour into our lives. Now, though, imagine someone has placed a plate over that cup. When you stumble into the kitchen with sleep-fogged eyes and pour out the coffeepot, the coffee will come out just fine—there's no problem with your coffeemaker—but instead of filling the cup, the hot, steaming liquid will flow onto the counter and floor. Or what if the coffee cup were already filled with stones when you tried to pour your coffee? Some of the coffee would still trickle down into the cup, but there wouldn't be any room for the full measure you were hoping to drink.

When we refuse to surrender our lives to God, they're like those coffee cups. His blessings are still there, still pouring out from Him—but we get in the way. We either block them out altogether, or we have so much in our lives already that we're holding on to that only a little of the blessings are able to trickle through.

The Bible is full of verses that promise God's blessings:

Fear not, O land; be glad and rejoice: for the LORD will do great things. (Joel 2:21 KJV)

It is the blessing of the LORD that makes rich, And He adds no sorrow to it. (Proverbs 10:22 NASB)

They will receive the LORD's blessing and have a right relationship with God their savior. (Psalm 24:5 NLT)

We used the coffee cup metaphor to describe how God's goodness is poured into our lives, but the author of Hebrews used another word picture to describe something similar: "For ground that drinks the rain which often falls on it and brings forth vegetation. . . receives a blessing from God" (6:7 NASB). That is exactly what God is longing to do in our lives: rain down His blessings, making us grow, making our lives productive, filling us with His goodness.

....

....

....

....

....

....

....

....

....

....

....

....

....

....

....

....

....

....

MAKE MY HEART LIKE AN EMPTY COFFEE CUP, LORD. FILL IT FULL WITH YOUR BLESSING.

GOD'S COMPASSION

Just as a father has compassion on his children, So the LORD has compassion on those who fear Him. For He Himself knows our frame; He is mindful that we are but dust.

PSALM 103:13-14 NASB

Surrendering ourselves to God doesn't come easily. It's a lifelong process. And it can't be accomplished by sheer willpower. As a result, sometimes we may feel as though God is withholding His goodness from us as a punishment for our lack of surrender to His will. That's not the way God works, though. The natural consequence of holding on to our lives, refusing to give them to God, is that we trip over our own feet. We prevent ourselves from being as effective and productive and creative as God longs for us to be. We shut ourselves off from the many ways that God longs to demonstrate His goodness to us and through us. But none of those are punishments from God. They're all things we do to ourselves.

Meanwhile, God understands our human nature (after all, He created us!), and He knows how hard it is for us to surrender to Him. He has compassion, and He is patient with our weakness. He knows we can't do anything without His help. The Bible tells us, "For God is working in you, giving you the desire and the power to do what pleases him" (Philippians 2:13 NLT).

Remember the man who told Jesus, "I do believe, but help me overcome my unbelief" (Mark 9:24 NLT)? Sometimes the best we can do is to pray something similar: "I want to surrender to You, God. Help me now to actually do it!" The author of Hebrews (13:20–21 MSG) put it like this:

> *May God, who puts all things together,*
> *makes all things whole,*
> *Who made a lasting mark through the sacrifice of Jesus,*
> *the sacrifice of blood that sealed the eternal covenant,*
> *Who led Jesus, our Great Shepherd,*
> *up and alive from the dead,*
> *Now put you together, provide you*
> *with everything you need to please him,*
> *Make us into what gives him most pleasure,*
> *by means of the sacrifice of Jesus, the Messiah.*
> *All glory to Jesus forever and always!*

GUIDANCE

Teach me thy way, O LORD, and lead me in a plain path.
PSALM 27:11 KJV

The Bible never pretends that it's easy to find God's way for our lives. Even thousands of years ago, when the Bible was written, human beings still struggled to know God and His will for them. They looked around and saw evil everywhere. They struggled to believe that God was truly good.

But throughout its pages, the Bible also promises that when we are surrounded by evil's darkness—even when this life's evil presses so close around that we can see nothing with our own eyesight—even then, God will guide our steps.

The book of Psalms is a good place to turn when we want an intimate glimpse into the spiritual struggles of one of the Bible's authors. "He will not suffer thy foot to be moved," the psalmist reminded himself; "he that keepeth thee will not slumber" (121:3 KJV). The Psalms are filled with prayers to God for guidance:

Lead me, O LORD, in thy righteousness because of mine enemies; make thy way straight before my face. (5:8 KJV)

Teach me thy way, O LORD; I will walk in thy truth: unite my heart to fear thy name. (86:11 KJV)

Cause me to hear thy lovingkindness in the morning; for in thee do I trust: cause me to know the way wherein I should walk; for I lift up my soul unto thee. (143:8 KJV)

We may not be able to see the path ahead, but God knows the way. He will keep us safe as we continue on life's journey, through the darkest days. We may not always be able to know He is there, but He will never forsake us. He leads us beside quiet waters, He refreshes our souls, and He guides us along the right paths. His goodness and love follow us all the days of our lives (Psalm 23:2–3, 6).

I NEED YOUR GUIDANCE TODAY, SHEPHERD OF MY SOUL. SHOW ME WHERE THE
QUIET WATERS AND GREEN PASTURES ARE. DIRECT MY PATH, I PRAY.

PRAYER

Don't worry about anything; instead, pray about everything.
Tell God what you need, and thank him for all he has done.

PHILIPPIANS 4:6 NLT

Imagine a good friend you talk to daily. You don't spend hours with her every day, but you set aside as much time as you can to spend together. Throughout the day, even while you're both busy with other things, you often send each other a quick text message or email, letting each other know that you're thinking of each other and informing one another of life's small joys and frustrations. If a crisis were to occur, you'd let her know immediately because you'd want her support and understanding.

Now imagine you shut down that open channel of communication between you and your friend. Days go by without the two of you communicating, and then weeks and even months. Before long you probably wouldn't feel as close to her. You might still care about her, but changes in both your lives would now come between you. You wouldn't know that she'd become a grandmother. She wouldn't know about the new job that takes up so much of your time now. As you no longer shared the important things in your lives, you would grow apart.

The same is true of our relationship with God. The only way to be close to Him is to spend time with Him and talk with Him often. The more we do that, the better we will come to know Him. As Paul knew, the more we pray, the less we'll worry. The more we thank Him for what He's done for us in the past, the more we'll trust Him for the future. Turning to Him constantly throughout the day will become habitual; it will seem like the natural way to live (and it is!). We'll share with Him all the details of our lives, and when emergencies come, we'll instantly reach out to Him.

"Let us come boldly to the throne of our gracious God," advises the writer of Hebrews. "There we will receive his mercy, and we will find grace to help us when we need it" (4:16 NLT). God wants to have a close and intimate friendship with us. He wants to keep the communication lines open, so that He fills our hearts with His goodness.

LET'S SPEND TIME TOGETHER TODAY, LORD. WE NEED TO TALK!

PRAYER AND JOY

Rejoice evermore. Pray without ceasing. In everything give thanks: for this is the will of God in Christ Jesus concerning you. Quench not the Spirit.
1 THESSALONIANS 5:16–19 KJV

Whether we surrender to God or try to cling to our own will, we really are powerless to control anything—but that doesn't stop us from trying to run the world. And yet that attitude seldom gives us any joy. It's far more likely to make us frustrated, angry, impatient, and resentful. In this verse from Thessalonians, Paul gives us practical advice for surrendering to God (and regaining our joy in the process). Basically, it comes down to this: pray all the time! If that doesn't seem possible to us, it's because we're not really understanding prayer.

Praying "without ceasing" doesn't mean we have a constant conversation going on with God inside our heads. It also doesn't mean that we've given up our jobs and our relationships with other and all the many daily concerns of our lives, so that we can sit somewhere alone and quiet, immersed in silent contemplation of the Lord. What it *does* mean is that the lines of communication between our hearts and God's are always open, no matter how busy we are. And it means that every time we notice ourselves trying to take back control of our lives (which is something we will probably do "without ceasing"!), we immediately hand them back to God.

Paul indicates that gratitude plays a part in this process as well. Saying thank You for all the circumstances in our lives is the way to surrender to His will at work. Thankfulness is a way to acknowledge the reality of God's goodness, even when it's hard to see. It restores our joy. It allows us to say:

Though the fig tree does not bud and there are no grapes on the vines, though the olive crop fails and the fields produce no food, though there are no sheep in the pen and no cattle in the stalls, yet I will rejoice in the LORD, I will be joyful in God my Savior. The Sovereign LORD is my strength; he makes my feet like the feet of a deer, he enables me to tread on the heights. (Habakkuk 3:17–19 NIV)

....
....
....
....
....
....
....
....
....
....
....
....
....
....
....
....
....

THANK YOU, GOD, FOR EACH THING YOU HAVE PUT IN MY LIFE—AND EACH THING
THAT YOU HAVE WITHHELD. YOU ARE MY STRENGTH. YOU GIVE ME JOY.

CARRIED

"There you saw how the LORD your God carried you, as a father carries his son, all the way you went until you reached this place."

DEUTERONOMY 1:31 NIV

Most of us are familiar with the poem called "Footprints in the Sand," where the author realizes that when she saw only one set of footprints it was because God was carrying her. It's a lovely reminder of God's kindness and goodness.

The Israelites needed the same assurance. After they left behind their slavery in the land of Egypt, they had traveled long years through the desert and wilderness. Now, the Promised Land lay ahead—but they couldn't believe it. Instead of trusting in the goodness of God, they "grumbled in their tents and said, 'The LORD hates us' " (Deuteronomy 1:27 NIV). Moses had to remind them that that wasn't the case at all. Instead, when their legs were too short and weak to keep going, God had picked them up and carried them, the way a parent carries a toddler.

The prophet Isaiah had a similar reassuring message for God's people. "He will carry the lambs in his arms," Isaiah wrote, "holding them close to his heart" (40:11 NLT). Later, Isaiah added:

Listen to Me, O house of Jacob. . .
You who have been borne by Me from birth
And have been carried from the womb;
Even to your old age I will be the same,
And even to your graying years I will bear you!
I have done it, and I will carry you;
And I will bear you and I will deliver you. (46:3–4 NASB)

When we start to doubt the goodness of God (when we find ourselves thinking, along with the Children of Israel, *The Lord hates me!*), we need to remind ourselves that God has not abandoned us. He has been carrying us ever since we were born—and He will continue to do so until our deaths.

LOVING GOD, THANK YOU THAT WHEN MY LEGS ARE TOO WEAK TO WALK, YOU CARRY ME.

WEARY BODIES

While we live in these earthly bodies, we groan and sigh, but it's not that we want to die and get rid of these bodies that clothe us. Rather, we want to put on our new bodies so that these dying bodies will be swallowed up by life.

2 CORINTHIANS 5:4 NLT

When we're young and healthy, we often take our bodies for granted. They do what we want them to do, for the most part, and we don't give them much thought. As we get older, though, sooner or later our bodies start to let us down. A long-lasting illness can hamper our ability to achieve the things we want to do. Instead of bounding out of bed filled with energy and eagerness to face a new day, stiff joints may turn even getting up in the morning into a painful experience that makes us groan.

Our physical conditions also shape how we see the world. When we feel well and strong, it's easier to praise God's goodness than when we are aching and weary. Pain in our bodies can cast a shadow over our entire lives, including our spirituality. It may be hard to perceive God's presence when we're tired and hurting.

We know that God's perfect plan for humanity didn't include illness or death—and one day, we will have new, eternal bodies that will never let us down. I wonder sometimes, though, if the aging process isn't also a sort of spiritual discipline that God has given us to teach us more about Him. As our bodies force us to reconsider who we are (not as strong and invincible as we once thought!), we can also come to know God better. Our bodies remind us that, in the words of the old song by Jim Reeves, "this world is not my home, I'm just a-passin' through."

Again and again, the Bible tells us to look at life with a kind of double vision, seeing the promise of eternity even in the midst of today's temporary pains. As Paul wrote, "So we don't look at the troubles we can see now; rather, we fix our gaze on things that cannot be seen. For the things we see now will soon be gone, but the things we cannot see will last forever" (2 Corinthians 4:18 NLT).

"He has planted eternity in the human heart," wrote the author of Ecclesiastes (3:11 NLT). Our weary bodies remind us that our true home is not in this world. "Now we see things imperfectly, like puzzling reflections in a mirror, but then we will see everything with perfect clarity. All that I know now is partial and incomplete, but then I will know everything completely, just as God now knows me completely" (1 Corinthians 13:12 NLT).

REST

Come with me by yourselves to a quiet place and get some rest.
MARK 6:31 NIV

Jesus and His disciples led busy lives. He wasn't the sort of spiritual guru who sat on the ground doing not much of anything. Instead, He was actively involved with the details of life. Perhaps He knew that His time was short and He had to make good use of every possible moment. In any case, Mark tells us in his Gospel that things had gotten so hectic that Jesus and His followers hadn't even had time to stop and eat.

We've all had times in our lives like that. So many people are coming at us from so many different directions, all with their own expectations and demands on our time and attention, that we feel guilty taking any time for ourselves. *Later,* we tell ourselves, *when life's not so busy, I'll take some time to get away and be quiet. But not now. I can't right now!*

But Jesus recognized that He and His followers needed a time of rest and quietness. "Let's get away for a while," He said to His friends. "Come with me to a quiet place I know. It will be just us; we won't tell the crowds where we're going. We need some time to rest" (Mark 6:31).

God gave a similar message to His people through the prophet Isaiah: "In repentance and rest is your salvation, in quietness and trust is your strength" (Isaiah 30:15 NIV). God knows that we can't keep serving Him if we don't take time to rest. Constant busyness robs us of our joy. It wears us down, emotionally, physically, and spiritually. God is still good—but we're too tired to feel His goodness! Taking time to run away from it all, to escape some place quiet, is the only thing that will save us and restore our strength.

Jesus is calling to us, maybe at this very moment, saying, "Come to Me, all who are weary and heavy-laden, and I will give you rest" (Matthew 11:28 NASB). We need to take His call seriously. It's an urgent and practical divine demand that's vital to our well-being, not something to be ignored or postponed. The author of Hebrews indicates this, writing, "Therefore, let us fear if, while a promise remains of entering His rest, any one of you may seem to have come short of it" (4:1 NASB).

....
....
....
....
....
....
....
....
....
....
....
....
....
....
....
....
....

JESUS, LET'S GO SOMEPLACE ALONE TODAY. I WANT TO REST IN YOUR PRESENCE.

INTERRUPTIONS

But as for me, I trust in You, O LORD, I say,
"You are my God." My times are in Your hand.

PSALM 31:14-15 NASB

We don't usually like interruptions. They often seem like pesky stumbling blocks thrown into our path. They trip us up; they keep us from getting everything done that we'd hoped to do. They may make us feel as though the world is specifically out to hinder us. We feel frustrated and irritated. Why would a good God allow our important work to be interrupted like this?

But the Bible asks us to trust in God's goodness even in the midst of life's trivial interruptions. When we are stuck in traffic, we can use those moments to tell God, "I trust in You. You are my God." We can choose to hear His voice calling to us through the toddler that interrupts our work to ask a thousand and one questions, in the telephone's ring, and in the neighbor who comes to our door when we're in the middle of something.

Our times are in God's hand. That means that His goodness is unfolding in ways we may not see. All those interruptions that slow us down—when we miss the elevator as we're rushing to be on time for an appointment, when we get stuck behind a slow driver, or when we find ourselves in a long line at the grocery store—might actually be God's voice calling to us.

If that's the case, then we are exactly where God wants us at that moment. If we can let go of our annoyance enough to look around a little, we may see something we would otherwise have missed—an elderly woman who needs some help, a child's smile, or a glimpse of sunlight through green leaves. Who knows what might be revealed to us if we allow ourselves to slow down a little?

Whenever little things interrupt our plans, we're also forced to accept that we're not actually in control of our lives. This means that interruptions are opportunities to practice surrendering ourselves to God by letting go of our frustration and saying, "Lord, my times are in Your hands."

GOD, I ASK THAT YOU GRANT ME THE GRACE TO HEAR YOUR VOICE WHISPERING THROUGH MY LIFE'S INTERRUPTIONS. I KNOW YOUR WAY FOR MY LIFE IS ALWAYS GOOD.

DISAPPOINTMENTS

This hope does not disappoint us, because God's love has been poured out into our hearts by the Holy Spirit, who has been given to us.

ROMANS 5:5 ISV

Disappointment comes in all shapes and sizes, big and small. We had hoped a family member would be able to come home for Christmas, and we're disappointed when we find out he can't get away. Or we had hoped our husband would give us a piece of jewelry for our birthday, and we're disappointed when instead we get a toaster. Maybe someone we counted on has let us down, and we're disappointed that this individual is not the person we had thought. Or maybe it's our own selves that have disappointed us. Our own failures and weaknesses have forced us to realize that we're not the people we dreamed of being.

Disappointments like these happen to everyone. Even the smallest disappointments can shake our confidence in God's goodness, but when we turn to the Bible, we read about person after person who hoped for something and then was disappointed. Abraham, Moses, David, the prophets—they all learned that disappointment is only temporary. What looked like a loss from a human perspective was eventually revealed to be the next step toward the amazing thing God was doing all along.

Disappointment can be another reminder to surrender ourselves more fully to God because whenever we cling to circumstances or people as our source of happiness, we are bound to be disappointed in the end. When we reach the point where we realize we have nothing to depend on but God, we can finally realize that His goodness is all we need.

That doesn't mean we'll never again be disappointed, nor will all our questions of "Why?" be answered in this life. But when we let go of some of the things we've set our hearts on, we make more room for the Holy Spirit to pour God's love into our lives.

Because no matter what else disappoints us, God never will! *The Message* expresses that promise like this:

We continue to shout our praise even when we're hemmed in with troubles, because we know how troubles can develop passionate patience in us, and how that patience in turn forges the tempered steel of virtue, keeping us alert for whatever God will do next. In alert expectancy such as this, we're never left feeling shortchanged. Quite the contrary—we can't round up enough containers to hold everything God generously pours into our lives through the Holy Spirit! (Romans 5:3–5)

···
···
···
···
···
···
···
···
···
···
···
···
···
···
···
···
···

THANK YOU, SPIRIT, THAT YOU WILL NEVER DISAPPOINT ME.

GETTING EVEN

"Do not seek revenge or bear a grudge against anyone among your people, but love your neighbor as yourself. I am the LORD."

LEVITICUS 19:18 NIV

When we first read this verse, we may dismiss it as one that doesn't relate to our own lives. After all, most of us probably wouldn't set out to physically injure someone who had hurt our feelings. We wouldn't throw eggs at their house or let the air out of their tires. We're far too good for that!

But what about when we're so mad at our husbands that we decide we're not going to talk to them until they say they're sorry for whatever they did. *That will teach him*, we think to ourselves. Or have we ever found ourselves being extra critical of someone who criticized us? Do we refuse to say hello to the neighbor who complained about our dog getting in his yard? Do we decide we won't call or email a family member who offended us at the last get-together?

If we do these things, we probably don't think of them as revenge. We feel we're justified in taking these small actions. The other person is in the wrong, we tell ourselves, and we're simply protecting ourselves against further hurt. Or we are teaching the other person a badly needed lesson about good manners. The questions we need to ask ourselves, though, are these: Are we treating the other person the way we would want them to treat us? Are we loving our neighbor (or our husband or family member) the way we love our own selves? That's the standard the Bible holds up to us.

Even if we don't act on our feelings, however, this verse from Leviticus tells us that from God's perspective, holding on to a grudge can be just as big of a problem. Resentful feelings damage our relationships with others—and with God. When our hearts are filled with anger, no matter how justified it may be, we can no longer experience the goodness of God. The statement in this verse that God is the Lord is yet another reminder to surrender ourselves more fully to God, allowing Him to be the Lord, in control of our lives rather than ourselves.

That doesn't mean, however, that when wrong is done, we're supposed to simply look the other way, nor does God ask us to "stuff" our emotions out of sight, like dirt swept under the carpet. Instead, we can give Him our hurt and anger. Rather than nursing our resentment, allowing it to grow and consume us the longer we dwell on it, we can ask that He give us insight into how we should handle the situation. And then we can wait to take action until we are certain we have His answer.

THANK YOU, GOD OF GRACE AND GOODNESS, THAT YOU CAN TRANSFORM EVERY
SITUATION. SHED YOUR LIGHT INTO MY HEART. ILLUMINE ALL
MY RELATIONSHIPS WITH YOUR LOVE.

RUNAWAY THOUGHTS

We take captive every thought to make it obedient to Christ.
2 CORINTHIANS 10:5 NIV

Thoughts are unruly things. We can sit down to pray—and two minutes later, realize that we're actually composing a grocery list in our heads. When we're lying in bed at night, unable to sleep, our thoughts can be particularly hard to curb. We want to focus on God's goodness, but instead, we find ourselves worrying about our kids. . .planning the next day's schedule. . . going over old painful memories. . .or being overwhelmed with a free-floating anxiety about everything and anything. People who meditate say that with practice we can get better at controlling what is sometimes called our "monkey mind," but that disobedient little monkey will never go away completely. So how can we take our thoughts captive? How can we make them obedient to Christ?

Martin Luther once said, "You can't keep the birds from flying over your head, but you can keep them from making a nest in your hair." What he meant by that is that anxious, angry, doubting thoughts will always enter our minds—but we can choose not to dwell on them. We don't have to pay attention to them and give them an ever-larger space in our heads. Instead, we can pick them up and put them briskly out the door.

Psychologists tell us we do that by replacing negative "self-talk" with positive. When we find ourselves thinking, *Why was I so stupid yesterday?* we can immediately replace the thought with, *I made a mistake yesterday but I can do better next time.* As Christians, we might want to also use scripture to counteract our negative thoughts. When we notice that we're dwelling on our worries about our wardrobe, for example, we might repeat Matthew 6:28: "Why take ye thought for raiment? Consider the lilies of the field, how they grow; they toil not, neither do they spin" (KJV). Or if we're sinking beneath anxiety over the future, we could remind ourselves: "There is surely a future hope for you, and your hope will not be cut off" (Proverbs 23:18 NIV). This is the tactic that Jesus used when He was tempted in the wilderness; He countered every suggestion from the devil with a quotation from scripture.

Although we can't stop thinking, we can control what thoughts occupy our minds. We can hold our thoughts accountable to the certainties of God's Word. Focusing on scripture will help us capture our thoughts and make them obedient to Christ.

JESUS, WHEN THOUGHTS ENTER MY MIND THAT CLOUD MY PERCEPTION OF
YOUR GOODNESS, HELP ME TO REPLACE THEM WITH YOUR TRUTHS.

FAILURE

Can anything ever separate us from Christ's love? Does it mean he no longer loves us if we have trouble or calamity, or are persecuted, or hungry, or destitute, or in danger, or threatened with death? . . . No, despite all these things, overwhelming victory is ours through Christ, who loved us.

ROMANS 8:35, 37 NLT

We all want to be successful. Countless books have been written on the topic, each one offering us yet another secret formula for guaranteeing that success will be ours. There are even books about how to be a "successful Christian."

There's nothing wrong with wanting to do a good job, and we often have the best of motives. We want to serve God and please Him. We want to help other people. We want our hard work to be effective and accomplish something. And all those sincere motives are often mixed up with other, less noble reasons for wanting to be successful—such as wanting to impress the world with how good we are, or longing to feel we are better than other people.

No matter how much we would prefer to be successful at everything we do, sooner or later we all fail at something. We make a mistake at work. We let others down when they're counting on us. We damage a relationship. We fail to live up to what God wants. We may blame others for our mistakes; we may even blame God. Other times we may get so afraid of failure that we refuse to try new things. Our fear paralyzes us. Failure can seem to separate us from God's love and goodness.

And yet everyone experiences failures. Even the great heroes of our Christian faith experienced their share of failure. Abraham and Moses, Elijah and David, Peter and Paul—they all knew what it was like to make serious mistakes. Abraham failed God when he fled to Egypt during the drought. Moses lost his temper and turned to violence more than once. David committed both adultery and murder. Peter denied Jesus.

God still used all these people who failed Him. In fact, He used even their failures to bring them to where He wanted them to be. He will do the same for us. No matter how many times we fail, His love never does. In the midst of our failures, we can still find victory in Christ.

Sometimes what the world considers failure is not failure at all from eternity's perspective. Remember, at first Jesus' disciples must have assumed that their leader's death on the cross was the worst failure of all. And yet what looked like failure brought new life to all creation.

....

....

....

....

....

....

....

....

....

....

....

....

....

....

....

....

....

LORD JESUS, EVEN IF MY EFFORTS OFTEN FAIL, HELP ME TO REMEMBER
THAT NOTHING EVER SEPARATES ME FROM YOUR LOVE.

LITTLE THINGS

"Leave her alone," said Jesus. "Why are you bothering her?
She has done a beautiful thing to me. . . . She did what she could."
MARK 14:6, 8 NIV

Many years ago, when I was in college, I went through a particularly bad time emotionally. As I walked around the quad one afternoon, snowflakes falling on my face, I felt as though I were drowning in despair. I hated myself. I was certain God must hate me too. How could He love someone as feeble and unlovely as I felt myself to be?

And then I saw a dark shape coming toward me through the snow. As he drew nearer, I recognized one of my professors. He looked into my face and gave me a smile so loving, so accepting of me, that without saying a word, he somehow showed me the love of Jesus. It was such a little thing, that smile, something I'm certain he never remembered later—but years later, I still remember the kindness in his face. It was the turning point for me emotionally; things didn't get magically better in my life, but now I felt the presence of God with me. I no longer felt separated from Him.

God uses the ordinary little things of life to reveal to us His goodness. A smile. . .a helping hand. . .a gentle word. . . these can make all the difference in life! When we doubt God's love, the tiniest act of kindness has the power to reassure us.

And like the woman who anointed Jesus' feet, we too "do what we can" to demonstrate our love for God. Mother Teresa has been credited with reminding us of this fact by saying, "Not all of us can do great things. But we can do small things with great love."

THANK YOU, LOVING LORD, FOR THE MANY LITTLE WAYS YOU SHOW ME YOUR LOVE.
HELP ME ALSO TO DO WHAT I CAN TO SHOW THE WORLD YOUR LOVE AND GOODNESS.

FRIENDS IN CHRIST

Saul's son Jonathan went to David. . .
and helped him find strength in God.
1 SAMUEL 23:16 NIV

In a book called *Life Together*, the German theologian Dietrich Bonhoeffer wrote:

> *The Christian needs another Christian who speaks God's Word to him. He needs him again and again when he becomes uncertain and discouraged, for by himself he cannot help himself without belying the truth. He needs his brother man as a bearer and proclaimer of the divine word of salvation.*[5]

This is the sort of relationship that David had with his friend Jonathan. Jonathan did not merely strengthen David with his friendship; instead, he pointed David to God as his source of strength.

Talking with a friend, sharing our lives, can help us draw closer to God. A faithful friend's words—even when we don't want to hear them!—can help us to look at our lives from God's perspective. She can hold up a mirror for us, so that we can see ourselves more clearly. And when God no longer seems good to us, a friend can show us the truth.

The gospel—the Good News of Jesus Christ—is made real through friendship. The kind of faith Jesus described can't be lived alone. Friendship is what gives Christ's Body strength; our relationships with others are the Church's bones and muscles. In these friendships, Christ's life is given flesh once again. We are His hands and feet.

We see God through our friends. God is present in their words and laughter, helping hands and sympathetic tears. He speaks to us through their voices. He loves us through them. Every time a friend sends us an encouraging email, takes time to sit and talk with us about a problem, prays with us, or calls us up just to say hello, we realize yet again—God is so good!

---

[5] Dietrich Bonhoeffer, *Life Together* (New York: Harper & Row, 1954).

JESUS, I'M SO GRATEFUL FOR THE "JONATHANS" YOU HAVE PUT IN MY LIFE!

HOUSEHOLD STRESS

O thou afflicted, tossed with tempest, and not comforted, behold, I will lay thy stones with fair colours, and lay thy foundations with sapphires.

ISAIAH 54:11 KJV

Family life is full of stress. Relationships, conflicting responsibilities, business—all of them contribute to the tension that often escalates within our homes. Family members' conflicting schedules get in the way of our closeness, and yet at the same time, simply sharing each other's space isn't always easy. We get on each other's nerves. We squabble over trivial things. We blame each other for all the stress in our households and fail to see how we ourselves contribute to it. And then it seems as though we're always hurrying out the door before we can have time to resolve our differences. When something out of the ordinary comes along—a death in the family, a job loss, a serious illness—the stress can mount to nearly unbearable levels. God may not look very good to us when our homes have become places of tension and strife!

Experts, however, say that while stress can be destructive, a certain amount of stress can also make us stronger. The same can be true of our families. There's no escaping some degree of household stress, but when we find ways to meet the challenges together, we draw closer to one another and to God.

What's more, God knows the stress that afflicts us, and He sees how upset we get—and all the while He is building a strong and beautiful foundation for our family's future. Each time we weather another crisis, we can thank God that He has guided our family through the storm. He will comfort us and make our home a beautiful place to be. God is so good to us!

DEAR LORD, I ASK FOR INSIGHT TO SEE WHICH PARTS OF MY FAMILY'S STRESSFUL SITUATION CAN BE CHANGED. SHOW ME THE UNHEALTHY HABITS THAT KEEP US CONSTANTLY STRESSED, AND GIVE US THE DETERMINATION TO BREAK THOSE HABITS TOGETHER.

THE GOOD SHEPHERD

The LORD is my shepherd; I shall not want.
PSALM 23:1 KJV

I've known the twenty-third Psalm by heart ever since my mother taught it to me when I was a little girl. As familiar as the words are, though, I don't always believe them, not deep down in my heart. I worry that instead of having everything I need, I'll be lacking the things I need and want most. I'm a lot like the woman Hannah Whitall Smith described in one of her books, who believed that

> . . .the Lord is the sheep, and I am the shepherd, and, if I do not keep a tight hold on Him, He will run away. When dark days came I never for a moment thought that He would stick by me, and when my soul was starving and cried out for food, I never dreamed He would feed me. I see now that I never looked upon Him as a good Shepherd at all.[6]

She went on to say, "Oh, no, I do not blame the Lord, but I am so weak and so foolish, and so ignorant, that I am not worthy of His care." To which, Hannah responded,

> But do you not know that sheep are always weak, and helpless, and silly; and that the very reason they are compelled to have a shepherd to care for them is just because they are so unable to take care of themselves? Their welfare and their safety, therefore, do not in the least depend upon their own strength, nor upon their own wisdom, nor upon anything in themselves, but wholly and entirely upon the care of their shepherd. And, if you are a sheep, your self also must depend altogether upon your Shepherd, and not at all upon yourself. . .either you have not believed He was your Shepherd at all, or else, believing it, you have refused to let Him take care of you. . . . You need not be afraid to follow Him whithersoever He leads, for He always leads His sheep into green pastures and beside still waters.[7]

"I am the good shepherd," Jesus told us. "The good shepherd lays down his life for the sheep" (John 10:11 NIV). Our Good Shepherd makes sure we have everything that we need. He leads us to sources of nourishment and refreshment. He gives us His very life.

---

[6] Hannah Whitall Smith, The God of All Comfort (Uhrichsville, OH: Barbour Publishing, 2013).
[7] Ibid.

....

....

....

....

....

....

....

....

....

....

....

....

....

....

....

....

....

SHEPHERD OF MY SOUL, THANK YOU FOR YOUR LOVE AND CARE. I KNOW I CAN TRUST YOU TO FEED ME, KEEP ME SAFE, AND GUIDE ME. YOU GIVE ME EVERYTHING I NEED.

GOD'S "MANNER OF LOVE"

Behold, what manner of love the Father hath bestowed upon us,
that we should be called the sons of God.

1 JOHN 3:1 KJV

John was one of Jesus' closest friends, so he knew from firsthand experience the "manner of love" God bestows on us. John had the privilege of seeing up close the relationship between Jesus and His Father, and through John's friendship with Jesus, he came to understand that God loves us with the tender, protective love of a parent for a child. We can trust Him to care for us the way a good parent cares for her children.

Often, though, we forget the loving, trusting relationship God extends to us.

Imagine if our young children stayed up late worrying about the family finances. We would tell them they didn't need to trouble themselves with that because it's our job to take care of them financially. Or what if our children constantly acted as though they were afraid of us, as though they thought we didn't really love them? Wouldn't we long to reassure them that we love them more than anything, that we would give our lives for them if necessary?

In the same way, God longs for us to feel secure in His love. He wants us to have confidence that because He is caring for us, we don't need to be anxious about anything. "This resurrection life you received from God is not a timid, grave-tending life," Paul reminded the Roman church. "It's adventurously expectant, greeting God with a childlike 'What's next, Papa?' God's Spirit touches our spirits and confirms who we really are. We know who he is, and we know who we are: Father and children. And we know we are going to get what's coming to us—an unbelievable inheritance!" (Romans 8:15–16 MSG). Paul wrote a similar message to the Galatians: "And because we are his children, God has sent the Spirit of his Son into our hearts, prompting us to call out, 'Abba, Father' " (Galatians 4:6 NLT).

This is the "manner of love" that God has for each of us. We are children of a good God!

ABBA GOD, SEND THE SPIRIT OF YOUR SON INTO MY HEART,
SO THAT I WILL BE CONVINCED THAT YOU ARE MY FATHER TOO.

GOD IS LOVE

God is love.
1 JOHN 4:8 NLT

John, the intimate friend of Jesus when He was on earth, was very clear about the divine nature. John had experienced it for himself, up close and personal, and he was confident he knew what he was talking about. He didn't need to write a complicated theological treatise about divine goodness because he knew just how simple it really was: God is love. That says it all.

John's simple three-word statement tells us that God has no selfishness; He doesn't hold Himself back from His creation; He keeps nothing to Himself. God's nature is to be always giving. In the words of the nineteenth-century reverend Andrew Murray, we see God's love "in the sun and the moon and the stars, in every flower you see it, in every bird in the air, in every fish in the sea." God communicates life and love to all creation.

Murray goes on to say,

And the angels around His throne, the seraphim and cherubim who are flames of fire—whence have they their glory? It is because God is love, and He imparts to them of His brightness and His blessedness. And we, His redeemed children—God delights to pour His love into us. And why? Because. . .God keeps nothing for Himself.[8]

Even God's three-person nature speaks to us of love, for, as Murray says, the Trinity is a revelation of divine love— "the Father, the loving One, the Fountain of love; the Son, the beloved one, the Reservoir of love, in whom the love was poured out; and the Spirit, the living love that united both and then overflowed into this world."

How can a God of love be anything but good? When we come to truly grasp the reality of His love, we will also finally know, without a shadow of doubt, that He is good!

---

[8] Andrew Murray, *Absolute Surrender and Other Addresses* (Chicago, IL: Moody Press, 1895).

160

GOD OF LOVE, I CAN'T COMPREHEND YOUR NATURE—BUT I DON'T NEED
TO. ALL I NEED TO DO IS ACCEPT THAT YOU ARE LOVE.

FRUITFUL

The fruit of the Spirit is love.
GALATIANS 5:22 KJV

"A new commandment I give unto you," Jesus said. "That ye love one another; as I have loved you, that ye also love one another" (John 13:34 KJV). We've all heard these Scripture verses; we know that as Christians we are supposed to love others—so we try to force ourselves to love. Being determined to act lovingly, out of sheer willpower, is better than not trying at all. After all, love has to be active and concrete to be real, and we can act in love even when our hearts don't feel particularly loving. But the Bible tells us that it doesn't need to be so hard.

God is so good that He has plenty of goodness to share with us. When His Spirit comes into us, He naturally reproduces His love in our hearts. "For we know how dearly God loves us," Paul wrote, "because he has given us the Holy Spirit to fill our hearts with his love" (Romans 5:5 NLT). George MacDonald wrote that God's love is "an indwelling power" that enters our hearts and then "leaps back to Him in love, and overflows" to others—"God's love to me, and my love to God, and my love to my fellow-men. The three are one; you cannot separate them."

The apostle John also had a lot to say about God's love. "No one has ever seen God," John wrote. "But if we love each other, God lives in us, and his love is brought to full expression in us" (1 John 4:12 NLT). In other words, when the Spirit enters our lives, He brings His love with Him—and the more we love others, the more the Spirit is able to express Himself within our hearts, in an endless cycle of renewal. Meanwhile, our love for others is what makes God visible in the world. God needs us to show the world His goodness.

And yet too often, those of us who claim Christ's name don't act very lovingly. We let differences of opinion come between us. We think our doctrines and theology are more important than love. We forget that God is love—and that if His Spirit has free rein in our lives, we will naturally overflow with love as well. If we don't, then there's something wrong.

LORD, SHOW ME ALL THE WAYS I GRIEVE YOUR SPIRIT BY NOT
LOVING. POINT OUT ANYTHING I NEED TO SURRENDER TO YOU,
ANYTHING THAT KEEPS ME FROM BEARING YOUR FRUIT.

LOVE'S RAINBOW

Love is patient, love is kind. It does not envy, it does not boast, it is not proud. It does not dishonor others, it is not self-seeking, it is not easily angered, it keeps no record of wrongs. Love does not delight in evil but rejoices with the truth. It always protects, always trusts, always hopes, always perseveres.

1 CORINTHIANS 13:4-7 NIV

Love is a small word that covers an immense scope of actions. In these verses, Paul breaks down love into some of its components. In the same way that we can shine light through a prism and break it into a rainbow of separate colors, Paul is separating love's elements into individual "colors," creating a "spectrum of love" that consists of the small and ordinary actions of which love is composed.

Here are the hues of Paul's love spectrum:

- Patience
- Kindness
- Freedom from envy
- Refusal to boast
- Humility
- Honoring others
- Avoiding self-seeking behaviors
- Turning away from anger
- Keeping no record of past wrongs
- Rejoicing in the truth
- Taking no pleasure in evil
- Protective
- Trusting
- Hopeful
- Persevering

Sometimes we may think of our faith as a separate, added-on thing, a piece of who we are that comes out on Sundays and when we're in the company of other Christians. Paul's love spectrum, however, tells us that our faith is to inspire our entire lives, transforming all our interactions with the practical reality of love's many hues.

And when we let this rainbow of love shine through our lives, we find God's presence illuminating our lives. We live in the midst of God, with His Spirit breathing through our lives. As we surrender our lives to His love, we will experience His goodness everywhere we turn.

GOD OF LOVE, SHINE YOUR LIGHT THROUGH MY LIFE. CREATE A RAINBOW OF LOVE IN ME.

LEARNING LOVE

We love, because he first loved us.

1 JOHN 4:19 NIV

Children learn to love by being loved. Their parents' love is what makes them able to love. They imitate their parents' loving behaviors, and discover the joys of loving and being loved. The same is true of us: we learn love from God. The more we soak up His love, the more loving we become. Love begets love.

God knows that love doesn't always come easily, though. Even the most affectionate of us have our selfish tendencies, the parts of ourselves that want to put our own needs and wishes ahead of others'.

We are generally motivated to become more loving to our friends and family. After all, we *love* them. We are aware that our love sometimes fails, that our selfishness trips us up and we hurt even the people we love most—but we usually try hard to do better. We pray for patience; we ask forgiveness for our anger and cruelty; we struggle to put these beloved people's needs ahead of ours. It's hard, but we try.

But what about the people we don't like—the people who annoy us, the people we don't respect, the people who believe things we find offensive, who act in ways that hurt our hearts? How can we love *those* people? Does God really expect us to? Isn't it enough if we love the people we're close to, and then simply avoid all the people we find so unlovable?

But that's not how God's love works. Divine love streams down on us all equally—and He wants us to be vehicles of that love, carrying it out into the world. And so He teaches us to love by loving us. When we feel unloving, the solution is to turn to God. The closer we are to Him, the more we surrender to Him, the more intimate we are with our Divine Lover, the more we will learn to love like He does. As we focus on Jesus, learning from the Gospels, we will see what love looks like in action. And as we daily open our hearts to God's presence, He will transform our lives, making them vehicles of His love and goodness.

TEACH ME TO LOVE, LORD. WHEN I SEE NOTHING LOVABLE IN THE OTHER PERSON,
SEND YOUR LOVE INTO MY HEART. AND WHEN I FIND IT HARD TO LAY ASIDE MY SELFISH
INTERESTS, REMIND ME THAT WHAT I NEED MOST IS TO SPEND MORE TIME WITH YOU.

SCARED!

*God is our refuge and strength, an ever-present help in trouble.
Therefore we will not fear, though the earth give way and
the mountains fall into the heart of the sea.*

PSALM 46:1–2 NIV

Fear is a normal and healthy biological reaction that alerts us to danger. Unfortunately, in our lives, fear and danger no longer necessarily go together. Instead, fear can exist all on its own. When that happens, fear becomes destructive and crippling.

Fear not only robs us of the goodness God wants us to experience in life, but it can also come between us and others. When we fear someone or something, we pull away. We put up barriers. Gandhi once said, "The enemy is fear. We think it is hate, but it is fear."

The commandment that is repeated more times in the Bible than any other is this one: "Fear not!" Scripture uses the precise words "fear not" or "be not afraid" 103 times, but it speaks about fear many more times than that. If you go online, you can find lists of "fear-not" verses for each day of the year. Bible scholars tell us that there are more than 500 verses in the Bible dealing with fear. Clearly, God doesn't want us to be afraid! He knows that fear can suck the goodness and love from our lives.

When we find ourselves in bondage to fear, He holds the key that can set us free. When life seems threatening, filled with unknown (and possibly imaginary) dangers, He will be our refuge. He is always there. In Him, we can always be secure. We can pray with the psalmist these words of power and comfort:

Lord, You are my light and my salvation. Whom shall I fear? You are the strength of my life. Of whom shall I be afraid? When my emotional enemies attack me, they'll stumble and fall. Though an entire army of fears come against me, my heart will be strong. Even in the midst of a war, I can be confident in You, because I ask You for only one thing: that I may dwell in Your house all the days of my life, seeing Your beauty. For I know that in the time of trouble, You will hide me in Your pavilion. You'll tuck me away in a secret nook inside Your tabernacle; You'll set me on a rock where I'll be safe, where I can lift up my head and see over the heads of my enemies. And that's why, Lord, I sing to You with joy! (Psalm 27:1–6, paraphrased)

....

....

....

....

....

....

....

....

....

....

....

....

....

....

....

THANK YOU, LORD, THAT BECAUSE YOU ARE GOOD, I HAVE NOTHING TO FEAR.
I CAN TRUST YOU. PLEASE TAKE ALL FEAR FROM ME AND REPLACE IT WITH YOUR LOVE.

HELPLESSNESS

"But the tax collector stood at a distance. He would not even look up to heaven, but beat his breast and said, 'God, have mercy on me, a sinner.'"

LUKE 18:13 NIV

We've all heard the expression, "God helps those who help themselves." And while there's a certain truth to the saying (God doesn't want us to sit there expecting a miracle when He's already put the means to accomplish something into our hands), the opposite is also true: God helps those who are helpless. Look at the tax collector who didn't even try to prove his worth. He just stood off at a distance and threw himself on God's mercy. Alcoholics Anonymous teaches that only when a person has hit bottom and finally acknowledged her helplessness is she ready to change.

In Jesus' day, the Pharisees didn't see themselves as helpless. They trusted in their own righteousness, in their own abilities to save themselves. But Jesus said, "Blessed are the poor in spirit, for theirs is the kingdom of heaven" (Matthew 5:3 NIV). When we have nothing left to cling to, we are truly helpless—but Jesus was telling us that when we give up our dependence on our own strength, then God can begin to act in our lives.

In helplessness, we can learn humility. We can surrender our pride and make more room for God's goodness in our lives. *The Message* writes Jesus' wise words like this:

You're blessed when you're at the end of your rope. With less of you there is more of God and his rule. You're blessed when you feel you've lost what is most dear to you. Only then can you be embraced by the One most dear to you. You're blessed when you're content with just who you are—no more, no less. That's the moment you find yourselves proud owners of everything that can't be bought. (Matthew 5:3–5)

The kind of helplessness that's rooted in false ideas about ourselves is not what Jesus is talking about here. He doesn't want us telling ourselves, *There's no way I can get out of this mess—it's hopeless*, or *There's nothing I can do to change this situation because I'm so weak. . .so lacking in skill. . .so unattractive. . .so unlovable. . .so stupid.* Jesus wants to fill us with His strength. He values every bit of who we are, and He wants to use all of it—the whole package—to bring His love into the world.

SOMETIMES, LORD JESUS, WHEN I FEEL HELPLESS, I'M REALLY JUST UNDERESTIMATING THE ABILITIES YOU'VE GIVEN ME. GIVE ME THE STRENGTH AND CONFIDENCE TO BECOME THE PERSON YOU CREATED ME TO BE. WITHOUT YOUR LOVE, MERCY, AND GOODNESS, I AM TRULY HELPLESS.

GREEDY!

"Beware! Guard against every kind of greed. Life is not measured by how much you own."

LUKE 12:15 NLT

We've often heard it said that money is the root of all evil. Actually, however, the Bible says that the *love of* money is the root of evil (1 Timothy 6:10). In other words, it's when we make money too important that we run into problems. Money itself is merely a useful tool, one that can be used for either good or bad.

Greed is the urge to get more and more of something, whether it be money or food or possessions. Greed—whether for financial riches, power, fame, food, or anything else—always gets us in trouble. The greedy person is too attached to the things of this world. And as a result, that person is often anxious, worried about losing what she already has.

Greed hurts others as well. When we put our desire for material things first in our lives, someone else often pays the price. Our greed also comes between our hearts and God's. The things that we desire turn into idols, taking the place that God wants in our lives. Material things never truly satisfy, though. Money, food, possessions, power—none of them are living things. Without God's Spirit using these things for His glory, these things are empty and lifeless.

Generosity is the opposite of greed. The Latin roots of this word have to do with being fruitful, producing life and energy; it's the same word roots as "generator"! Greed is a dead thing, but generosity opens us to the creative fruitfulness of God's Spirit. The generous person is grateful for the good things God brings into her life. And she can just as easily let them go. It gives her joy to share, and loss doesn't worry her. She knows that God has plenty to give her, and His grace will never be exhausted.

THE TURNING POINT

Thus says the Lord GOD, "Repent and turn away from your idols and turn your faces away from all your abominations."

EZEKIEL 14:6 NASB

The dictionary definition of "repent" is to be sorry for our sins—but in Hebrew, "turn" or "return" is the literal meaning of the word that our English Bibles often translate as "repent." The Bible says that repentance is an action, not a feeling. It tells us clearly what this action looks like: "Stop doing wrong. Learn to do right; seek justice. Defend the oppressed" (Isaiah 1:16–17 NIV).

We can see what repentance looks like when we read Peter's story. Peter had many wonderful qualities. He left his old life behind and followed Jesus (Matthew 19:27). He was quick to obey his Master's instructions, even if it meant doing the impossible, like walking on water (Matthew 14:28). Peter also had deep spiritual insight. When Christ asked the disciples: "Whom say ye that I am?" Peter was able to answer: "Thou art the Christ, the Son of the living God" (Matthew 16:15–16 KJV). Jesus recognized and loved all these qualities in Peter—but Jesus also knew that Peter had not truly died to self. As much as Peter loved Jesus, he wasn't ready to follow Jesus to the cross. When push came to shove, Peter denied his Lord.

But that's not the end of Peter's story. The Gospel tells us that when Peter realized what he had done, he "went out, and wept bitterly" (Luke 22:62). He was ashamed and sorry. That wasn't enough, though. The turning point in his life came after the Resurrection, when he and Jesus were on the beach by the Lake of Galilee (John 21). There, Jesus told Peter the action he needed to take now, the new direction he needed to go if he truly loved Jesus: "If you love me, then feed my lambs," Jesus said.

What did Jesus mean by this? He meant that Peter had to turn around completely and head in a new direction. Instead of putting himself first, now he had to focus on others. He had to follow the example of the Good Shepherd, and put others' needs ahead of his own.

And Peter did. In the letters that Peter wrote later, he showed that he had been transformed by Jesus' love. I "am an apostle on assignment by Jesus, the Messiah," he wrote. "May everything good from God be yours! . . . Because Jesus was raised from the dead, we've been given a brand-new life and have everything to live for, including a future in heaven—and the future starts now!" (1 Peter 1:1, 4 MSG).

CALL TO ME, LORD, WHENEVER I START HEADING IN THE WRONG
DIRECTION, AWAY FROM YOU AND YOUR GOODNESS.

175

SECRET SIN

"People look at the outward appearance,
but the LORD looks at the heart."

1 SAMUEL 16:7 NIV

If sin is anything that comes between God and us, then we are simply deceiving ourselves if we think there's any point in burying our sins out of sight where no one can see them. Sin that is hidden still gets in the way of our relationships with God. By hiding it out of sight, we may think we have fooled other people. We may even fool ourselves. We do not fool God.

In the Gospels, Jesus makes clear that our hidden thoughts are just as serious and damaging as our external behaviors. He wants us to be people of integrity and wholeness, without any darkness festering inside us. He knows that ultimately, it is our own selves that are hurt most by these shameful secrets.

God's Word tells us that He will one day judge the secrets of every heart (Romans 2:16). He will bring everything to judgment, everything which is hidden, whether good or evil (Ecclesiastes 12:14). In the Gospels, Jesus said that everything that is covered up will be revealed, and everything that's hidden will be known. The things we think we said when we were alone, with no one listening, will be proclaimed from the housetops (Luke 12:2–3). How embarrassing!

Even worse, though, is the way in which our secret sins come between us and the good God wants to manifest in our lives. Those tiny, unimportant, little sins we've hidden away inside our hearts can cast dark shadows, getting in the way of God's light. We're far better off without them!

EXAMINE MY HEART, LOVING LORD. MAY THERE BE NO SECRETS BETWEEN US.
CLEAN OUT MY HEART. AS I GAZE INTO THE MIRROR OF YOUR WORD,
REVEAL TO ME ANYTHING THAT COMES BETWEEN US.

INJUSTICE

The LORD loves righteousness and justice;
the earth is full of his unfailing love.

PSALM 33:5 NIV

We live in a world of injustice. A third of all the children in the world's developing nations suffer from malnutrition. Almost three million children die each year from hunger. This isn't fair. It's not just. How can a good God allow these things to exist?

The Bible makes clear, however, that justice is important to God. In the Gospels, Jesus talks more about justice for those who are poor than He does about violence or sexual immorality. In fact, about a tenth of all the verses in the four Gospels have to do with concern for the poor.

Scripture is emphatic that it's our job to bring God's justice to an unjust world. He doesn't want us to look away from the world's injustice. He wants us to face it—and fight it. He says to us, "Attend to matters of justice. Set things right between people. Rescue victims from their exploiters. Don't take advantage of the homeless, the orphans, the widows. Stop the murdering!" (Jeremiah 22:3–4 MSG).

God calls us to share what we have with those who have less than us (Proverbs 22:16). He asks us to be kind to strangers, to those who are aliens in our land (Exodus 22:21). He reminds us to treat with respect those who have apparently lower positions than we do (Job 31:13–14).

But sometimes we confuse justice with vengeance. We think that justice means that bad people need to get "what they deserve." The Bible, however, tells us to leave all that to God rather than take it upon ourselves (Hebrews 10:30). We are to help the victim, to work to put an end to all that is unfair in our world—but we are not to personally mete out punishment to the perpetrators. Instead of getting even when we're injured, Jesus tells us to turn the other cheek (Matthew 5:39).

....
....
....
....
....
....
....
....
....
....
....
....
....
....
....
....
....
....

HELP ME TO ALWAYS FOLLOW YOUR EXAMPLE, JESUS, WORKING FOR JUSTICE
IN PRACTICAL WAYS. USE ME TO REVEAL YOUR GOODNESS IN OUR WORLD.

TOO WEAK TO KEEP GOING

But those who trust in the LORD will find new strength. They will soar high on wings like eagles. They will run and not grow weary. They will walk and not faint.

ISAIAH 40:31 NLT

There are so many demands on our strength. So many crises to confront, so many problems to solve, so many people who need our help. We feel exhausted. We're not sure we can go on. Some days, we'd like to just give up. We've reached the end of our strength. God may be good—but our weakness seems greater than His goodness.

And yet when we acknowledge our own weakness, that's the exact moment when the Holy Spirit can begin to work in our lives in new ways. When we throw up our own hands, God's hands have room to work.

The author of Hebrews reminds us that through Jesus, we have direct access to God, the Creator of the universe. When we feel too weak to keep going, we just need to avail ourselves of this amazing resource that is our Lord.

Now that we know what we have—Jesus, this great High Priest with ready access to God—let's not let it slip through our fingers. We don't have a priest who is out of touch with our reality. He's been through weakness and testing, experienced it all—all but the sin. So let's walk right up to him and get what he is so ready to give. Take the mercy, accept the help. (4:14–16 MSG)

The Bible is full of other assurances we can turn to when we feel too weak to go on. It promises that we can do all things through God who gives us strength (Philippians 4:13), that our strength comes from God's might (Ephesians 6:10), that the Spirit will help us when we are weak (Romans 8:26), and that God's grace will always be enough for us, giving us the strength we need to keep going even when it seems impossible (1 Corinthians 12:9).

YOU KNOW MY WEAKNESS, LORD. REPLACE IT WITH YOUR STRENGTH.

GOD'S FRIENDSHIP

Henceforth I call you not servants; for the servant knoweth not what his lord doeth: but I have called you friends; for all things that I have heard of my Father I have made known unto you.

JOHN 15:15 KJV

The goodness of God is demonstrated to us in this verse. Jesus thinks of us as His friends! The Son of God wants to enter in to an intimate relationship between equals with us. How amazing is that?

"You are people who are dear to Me," Jesus was saying to us, "people I think of as My equals." He was not communicating with His disciples as a superior does with his inferiors. A servant and master cannot be equals. Friends, however, speak openly with each other on equal footing. They trust each other without reserve. They share their plans and goals with each other, and they talk over that which is most important to them. This is the sort of friendship Jesus had with His disciples (and the sort of friendship He wants to have with us as well).

Webster's dictionary tells us that our word *friend* comes from Old English roots that meant both to love and to free. That is what friendship does: it ties us together with love even while it sets us free to be uniquely ourselves. Jesus understood that friendship is squelched by feelings of superiority or possessiveness. Real friends know they don't exist purely for the other's benefit. They respect each other's separate interests. They work to protect and defend each other's rights. They don't try to own or control each other. They don't lord it over each other or try to make the other one feel inferior in some way. This is how Jesus treats us, sharing with us all that He receives from the Father.

Do we think of our friends as our equals? Or do we ever think of them more as servants, put in our lives for our convenience? Christ wants us to love our friends enough to set them free. He wants us to show them the same friendship He extends to us.

ABSENT?

My God, my God, why have you forsaken me? Why are you so far from saving me, so far from my cries of anguish?

PSALM 22:1 NIV

Sometimes God allows a period of pain and hardship in our lives, a long space where we start to wonder if our walk with God has been just a figment of our imaginations. We begin to doubt His existence—or if we still believe in God, we wonder if He really loves us after all. He seems so far removed from our lives. We can't feel His presence. We can't see His hand at work in our lives. He doesn't seem like a good God at all!

Sometimes, to add insult to injury, we even beat ourselves up for feeling this way. As women, we're good at blaming ourselves! It must be our fault if we can't feel God, we tell ourselves. If we were more spiritual, more disciplined, better in some way. . . .

Even Jesus experienced these same feelings. On the cross, He asked His Father, "Why did You leave Me?" (Matthew 27:46). Jesus understands our feelings—and He never condemns us for feeling them.

God answers our fears with promises that He will never leave us, no matter what our cloudy perceptions may seem to say. As proof of this, He tells us, "Look! I have written your name on My hand" (Isaiah 49:16).

I love this image of God's love. It reminds me of when I was a teenager and I wrote the name of the boy I liked on the palm of my hand. My fingers closed around his name like a hug. His name on my skin made me feel closer to him when we weren't together. What a silly thing to do! But the God who created the universe loves us like that. He's silly with love over us.

God is never absent. We can believe in His goodness, still present in our lives even when we don't *feel* it. He has promised He will never, ever leave us.

LOVING LORD, WHEN I FEEL AS THOUGH YOU HAVE LEFT ME ALL ALONE,
REMIND ME THAT MY NAME IS WRITTEN ON YOUR HAND.

ONLINE

I love the LORD because he hears my voice and my prayer for mercy. Because he bends down to listen, I will pray as long as I have breath!
PSALM 116:1–2 NLT

When I sit down at my computer, I often glance at my Facebook page to see which of my friends are online. Sometimes we message each other back and forth throughout the day. The internet, despite all its faults, is a wonderful vehicle for friendship and connection.

When it comes to our connection to our Heavenly Friend, He is always "online," always waiting for us to post an update or send a message. That's what prayer is. It's the simple, easy connection that comes through a spiritual "internet" that is never down but is always available to us.

The Bible doesn't tell us that we have to pray in a certain way in order to find God. It doesn't teach that we have to follow an elaborate prayer discipline or practice certain techniques. That's not to say that certain disciplines can't be helpful to our spiritual lives, but when it comes right down to it, the Bible makes clear that prayer is very simple. All we have to do is look for God—and whether we can sense His presence with us or not, there He is! It's the very act of turning toward God, the opening ourselves to His potential and power, that is the truest, most basic form of prayer.

Prayer is as simple as the moment when we cry, "Help!" It is the acknowledgment that our own strength is not enough, that we're willing to let go of our own control of our lives and trust that God is good. Sometimes we may express our prayers in words, sometimes in song. We may be on our knees or facedown on our beds. But God hears us just as well if we're driving in our cars, sitting at our computers, or in the midst of a conversation with a friend.

"Let us come boldly to the throne of our gracious God," advises the writer of Hebrews. "There we will receive his mercy, and we will find grace to help us when we need it" (4:16 NLT). God promises that if we seek Him, we will find Him. He's always online with our hearts—and He doesn't need a bell or a special signal to bring His attention to us. He's always there, ready to listen, ready to help. All we have to do is turn toward Him.

I AM SO GRATEFUL, GOD, THAT YOU ARE ALWAYS THERE, WAITING FOR MY MESSAGES.
THE CONNECTION BETWEEN US IS ALWAYS OPEN ON YOUR END.

SLEEPLESS

He grants sleep to those he loves.
PSALM 127:2 NIV

Insomnia is a terrible thing. When we're tired, we're more likely to feel anxious or depressed, more easily angered, less patient. It becomes a vicious circle: the more upset and tense we become, the less we can sleep; the less we sleep, the more upset and tense we become. We may end up afraid to even go to bed because we don't want to face the frustration of laying there awake again. Anxiety overwhelms us in the darkness. We feel helpless, tense. In the midst of all that, God may not look too good to us. We don't need theology or religion; we need sleep!

When we have a living relationship with God (rather than a formal religion we take out on Sundays), however, we start to understand that God is present in *all* our needs, including our need for rest. Each thing that happens to us—even insomnia—is an opportunity to experience God's goodness in a new way. The Bible tells us that God has compassion on our sleeplessness. His love never fails. He is with us there in the darkness. So the next time you lie awake, tossing and turning and trying to relax, reread these words from God:

You can go to bed without fear; you will lie down and sleep soundly. (Proverbs 3:24 NLT)

In peace I will both lie down and sleep, For You alone, O LORD, make me to dwell in safety. (Psalm 4:8 NASB)

I was crying to the LORD with my voice, And He answered me from His holy mountain. Selah. I lay down and slept; I awoke, for the LORD sustains me. I will not be afraid. (Psalm 3:4–6 NASB)

Remember the Gospel story about the time that the disciples and Jesus were caught in a terrible storm at sea (Matthew 8:24)? The waves were so high that they were washing over the decks, and the disciples must have been terrified. To their amazement, they found Jesus sleeping peacefully, as though the water was completely calm.

The "moral of the story" isn't that God is sleeping when we are in danger. Instead, Jesus was telling his friends that there was nothing for them to worry about. It reminds me of falling asleep as a child in the backseat of the family car, trusting absolutely in my father's ability to steer through the darkness. In the same way, we don't need to be anxious and sleepless, no matter how fierce the storms in our life. We can relax, knowing God is in charge.

WORK TENSION

Work willingly at whatever you do, as though you were working for the Lord rather than for people.

COLOSSIANS 3:23 NLT

Our jobs are often the source of much of the stress in our lives. Tight deadlines, multiple responsibilities, conflicts with coworkers and supervisors—all these can lead to tension that interferes with our sensitivity to the goodness of God. Since we're likely to spend about half our lives in our workplaces, though, we need to find joy and satisfaction, rather than stress and anxiety, in our jobs.

We can learn to sense God's presence with us as we work. Even on our busiest days, we need to find ways to direct our attention to God. Here are a few suggestions:

- When you first sit down at your desk or pick up whatever your work tools are, say to God, "Use my hands today. May the work I do please You."
- Instead of using break time or lunch hours to socialize with coworkers, take a few moments first to go for a walk or sit in a quiet place. Use those moments to reorient your attention on God.
- Set a timer on your phone, watch, or computer that reminds you once an hour to pause and take thirty seconds to spend in prayer. That tiny space of time won't interfere with your work productivity. It may even increase it!
- Be aware of the words you speak to your colleagues and supervisors. Remember that you represent Jesus. Do your best to speak only peace and grace to everyone with whom you interact.
- At the end of each workday, before you go home, pause again for a moment and consciously place in God's hands all that you accomplished during the day—as well as all that is still undone.

Ultimately, we need to remember that we are not working only for a paycheck or for our own satisfaction. We are working for Jesus.

....
....
....
....
....
....
....
....
....
....
....
....
....
....
....
....

LORD, I PRAY THAT YOU WILL USE MY WORK. MAY I FIND GLADNESS IN MY EFFORTS,
AND MOST OF ALL, MAY I PLEASE YOU.

JOURNAL YOUR WAY TO A DEEPER FAITH

Today God Wants You to Know...You Are Beautiful Devotional Journal

This beautiful women's devotional journal will delight and encourage you in your daily faith walk, as though you are hearing messages straight from God Himself through His Word.

Paperback / 978-1-64352-072-8 / $14.99

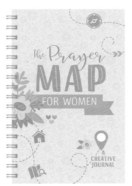

The Prayer Map for Women

This engaging prayer journal is a fun and creative way for you to more fully experience the power of prayer in your life. Each page features a lovely 2-color design that guides you to write out specific thoughts, ideas, and lists. . .which then creates a specific "map" for you to follow as you talk to God.

Spiral Bound / 978-1-68322-557-7 / $7.99